Twayne's New Critical
Introductions to Shakespeare

By the same author

*The Carbon Copy* (Toronto: McClelland and Stewart, 1973)
*The Crazy House* (Toronto: McClelland and Stewart, 1975)
*Shakespeare's Dramatic Structures* (London: Routledge and Kegan Paul, 1986)
*Onstage and Offstage Worlds in Shakespeare's Plays* (London: Routledge, 1989)

# Twayne's New Critical
# Introductions to Shakespeare

# HENRY V

Anthony Brennan

TWAYNE PUBLISHERS · NEW YORK
An imprint of Macmillan Publishing Co.

Published in the United States by Twayne Publishers,
imprint of Macmillan Publishing Co.,
866 Third Avenue, New York, NY 10022

Published simultaneously in Great Britain by
Harvester Wheatsheaf
Campus 400, Maylands Avenue, Hemel Hempstead, Herts.

Twayne's New Critical Introductions to Shakespeare, no. 16

## Library of Congress Cataloging-in-Publication Data

Brennan, Anthony.
    Henry V / Anthony Brennan.
       p.   cm. – (Twayne's new critical introductions to Shakespeare:
    no. 16)
    Includes bibliographical references and index.
    ISBN 0-8057-8731-3. – ISBN 0-8057-8732-1 (pbk.)
    1. Shakespeare, William, 1564-1616.  Henry V.  2. Henry V,
King of England, 1387-1422, in fiction, drama, poetry, etc.   3.
Great Britain—History—Henry V, 1413-1422—Historiography.
4. Kings and rulers in Literature.   I. Title.   II. Series.
PR2812.B74   1992
822.3′3—dc20                                                    92-26948
                                                                      CIP

# Titles in the Series

## GENERAL EDITOR: GRAHAM BRADSHAW

# General Editor's Preface

The *New Critical Introductions to Shakespeare* series will include studies of all Shakespeare's plays, together with two volumes on the non-dramatic verse, and is designed to offer a challenge to all students of Shakespeare.

Each volume will be brief enough to read in an evening, but long enough to avoid those constraints which are inevitable in articles and short essays. Each contributor will develop a sustained critical reading of the play in question, which addresses those difficulties and critical disagreements which each play has generated.

Different plays present different problems, different challenges and excitements. In isolating these, each volume will present a preliminary survey of the play's stage history and critical reception. The volumes then provide a more extended discussion of these matters in the main text, and of matters relating to genre, textual problems and the use of source material, or to historical and theoretical issues. But here, rather than setting a row of dragons at the gate, we have assumed that 'background' should figure only as it emerges into a critical foreground; part of the critical endeavour is to establish, and sift, those issues which seem most pressing.

So, for example, when Shakespeare determined that *his* Othello and Desdemona should have no time to live together, or that Cordelia dies while Hermione survives, his deliberate departures from his source material have a critical significance which is often blurred, when discussed in the context of lengthily detailed surveys of 'the sources'. Alternatively, plays like *The Merchant of Venice* or *Measure for Measure* show Shakespeare welding together different 'stories' from quite different sources, so that their relation to each other becomes a matter for critical debate. And Shakespeare's dramatic practice poses different critical questions when we ask – or if we ask: few do – why particular characters in a poetic drama speak only in verse or only in prose; or when we try to engage with those recent, dauntingly specialised and controversial textual studies which set out to establish the evidence for authorial revisions or joint authorship. We all read *King Lear* and *Macbeth*, but we are not all textual critics; nor are textual critics always able to show where their arguments have critical consequences which concern us all.

Just as we are not all textual critics, we are not all linguists, cultural anthropologists, psychoanalysts or New Historicists. The diversity of contemporary approaches to Shakespeare is unprecedented, enriching, bewildering. One aim of this series is to represent what is illuminating in this diversity. As the hastiest glance through the list of contributors will confirm, the series does not attempt to 'reread' Shakespeare by placing an ideological grid over the text and reporting on whatever shows through. Nor would the series' contributors always agree with each other's arguments, or premises; but each has been invited to develop a sustained critical argument which will also provide its own critical and historical context – by taking account of those issues which have perplexed or divided audiences, readers, and critics past and present.

Graham Bradshaw

# Contents

# Preface

*Henry V* has been regarded for most of its history as a workman-like stage pageant celebrating a great king and the British lads who helped him achieve a miraculous victory at Agincourt. It has been used as a piece of straightforward propaganda to be rolled out at coronations, times of national crisis, and in any other circumstance when the British feel inclined to burst their buttons with pride. As such it seemed untypical of the complexities usually found in Shakespeare's work and often irritated those resistant to its apparent patriotic message. The complacent jingoism promoted for three centuries by the radical editing of Shakespeare's text began to be questioned about forty years ago. Where the play had once been a reliable, unproblematical, and not especially challenging tapestry of famous events it gradually became an exciting, complex, ambiguous and disturbing account which seemed fully responsive to current political anxieties. The reputations of many of Shakespeare's plays have been modified in this century but in none has the transformation been quite as complete as in *Henry V*. Many scholars have rallied round the flag to salvage Henry's reputation as the admirable Boy Scout audiences had warmed to for centuries. In recoiling from Henry-hero, revisionist productions have often over-compensated with a hatchet job that has aroused the wrath of theatre critics. In my account of this play I have been indebted to a wide range of probing, stimulating analyses which the play has recently called forth. I have placed a great deal of emphasis on the details of stage productions and on the variety of ways in which the text has been cut for theatre presentation, for it is in the theatre that the excitement involved in its re-examination has been most vividly expressed. I come neither to bury Henry nor to praise him. Scarcely ever in the past nor even now in revised interpretations is the whole text presented on stage. My chief aim is to suggest a balanced and consistent approach to the remarkable complexities of Shakespeare's view of *Henry V*, which can only be achieved by an examination of *all* the text.

# Acknowledgements

I would like to acknowledge my gratitude to the Social Sciences and Humanities Research Council of Canada and the Arts Research Board of McMaster University for the funding which allowed me to undertake the research for this volume. I register also my sincere thanks to the staffs of the Shakespeare Centre Library in Stratford-upon-Avon, England and of the Theatre Archives of the Festival in Stratford, Ontario. In the text all productions in Stratford-upon-Avon, England are designated by SE and the year of the production, whether they occurred before or after the founding of the Royal Shakespeare Company. All productions at Stratford, Ontario are designated SO with the date, and those at Stratford, Connecticut SC with the date. The full publication details of the bracketed references to the work of other critics are to be found in the Select Bibliography. In line with other volumes in the series all quotations from *Henry V* and other Shakespearian plays are from William Shakespeare, *The Complete Works*, ed. Peter Alexander, London, 1951.

# Stage History

Productions of the play until the last fifty years were, with few exceptions, radically cut and rearranged, presented as a patriotic hymn, employed in times of war as a kind of recruiting poster, and varying only in the amount of elaborate spectacle for which the play could be considered an excuse. In summarising the details of productions before this century I am indebted to the work of Agate, Brewster, Cole, Coleman, Foulkes, Hogan, Odell, Spanabel, Sprague and Trewin.

England's warrior-king was a popular subject among the Elizabethans for there were at least three plays about him between 1587 and 1598. Shakespeare finished his play by June 1599 and its first performance must have come later that year. That someone acquired and printed a version of the play in an unauthorised text in 1600, and reprinted it in 1602, implies that it had some popularity. The Revels Account records a performance at court on 7 January 1605, so that it was evidently in the company's repertoire for at least six years. The deeds of Henry V remained popular throughout the century. Pepys saw Betterton's conflation of 2 *Henry IV* with parts of *Henry V* in 1668, but after the initial success of this adaptation, the play fell out of favour for an extended period.

In 1720 *The Half-Pay Officers*, attributed to Charles Molloy, appeared, an odd compilation of situations, characters and speeches from *Henry V*, *Much Ado About Nothing*, Davenant's *Love and Honour* and Shirley's *The Wedding*. The author stole outright the character of Fluellen and some of the dialogue of Macmorris, and adapted his character Culverin from Pistol. Another adaptation of the play by Aaron Hill, which has been called 'the last of these historical murders' (Odell, 1966, p. 252), appeared in 1723 and was revived in 1735–6 and 1746. Hill uses fourteen speaking roles, twelve of them from Shakespeare. He introduces 'gentle Harriet', Scroop's niece, who aids in her uncle's conspiracy to kill the king in revenge for his neglected love of her. Disguised throughout as a boy, she visits Princess Katharine and the Dauphin to enlist their aid in the plot. Touched, however, by Henry's assertions of undiminished love and the burdens of his duties, Harriet reveals the conspiracy and then stabs herself. While the battle of Agincourt is conducted offstage the Genius of England rises and obliges with a song. At times Hill borrows entire speeches from Shakespeare, adapts them and transfers them from one scene or character to another. Henry's soliloquy on Ceremony is given to Katharine. The Chorus is replaced by a prologue and fragments of his speeches distributed throughout to other characters. Because such a serious subject as majesty should not, according to eighteenth-century notions of decorum, be sullied by anything 'low' the roles of Pistol, Nym, Bardolph, Fluellen and Macmorris are cut, iii.iv omitted, and Henry's courtship of Katharine (v.ii) passed over for more kingly behaviour.

In the plays produced in London between 1701 and 1800 *Henry V* received only 142 performances and was eighteenth in popularity. The first recorded production of Shakespeare's play after the 1605 performance at court was at Covent Garden on 23 February 1738, and the advertisement noted it was 'Not acted these forty years' to stress the significance of the revival. Dennis Delane played the role in the 1738 revival and continued intermittently in the role until his death in 1750. In the fevered response to the fourth attempt of the century by the Stuarts to capture England's throne the play was used, on the first of many occasions, for political purposes. Notices of performances in 1744 and 1745 usually included phrases such as 'the glorious victory of the English over the French', encouraging audiences to see the Agincourt of 1415 in the light of a contemporary defeat of the

French army. A one-act version of the play, *The Conspiracy Discovered*, performed in 1746, related the Cambridge conspiracy (II.ii) to that of three figures in the Jacobite rebellion. In the productions at Drury Lane, 1747–50, Garrick chose not to challenge Spranger Barry in the title role and performed the role of Chorus instead. Macklin was noted for his performance of Fluellen. Barry moved to Covent Garden, where he played the role seven times (1750–8). William 'Gentleman' Smith became dominant in the role at Covent Garden, playing it fifty-seven times between 1755 and 1779, a record not broken until 1859 when Charles Kean played the role eighty-four times. Acting editions of the time often omit the Chorus, though Garrick's performance must have given some force to the role. The Bell edition of 1773 cuts all the Choruses but the Prologue, III.iv, which Gentleman thought of a 'trifling, childish nature, disgraceful to the author and the piece', and shortens most of the longer speeches throughout the play. At the coronation of George III in 1761 a dramatic representation, *The Procession from the Abbey at the Coronation*, was offered by the Covent Garden manager, John Rich, and thereafter was attached to all performances of *Henry V* until 1769. The association of the play with royal celebrations and other occasions of national pride has persisted up to the present.

Kemble first produced the play in his second season of management at Drury Lane in 1789 in a heavily edited text. During the period in which he was presenting the play England was at war for much of the time with France. The receipts for the performance of 25 November 1789 were given to the Patriotic Fund. Following the final curtain Charles Kemble spoke an 'Occasional Address to the Volunteers' which brought applause and a singing of 'God save the King' by the cast. In 1789 Kemble cut 1,460 lines (43.3 per cent), and in his final production in 1811, 1,404 lines (41.6 per cent). With minor variations he followed the major omissions of the Bell text: all Choruses, the clerics' discussion of Henry's moral reformation (I.i), the list of French kings and the honey-bees speech (I.ii), the king's anger at the traitors (II.ii), most of III.i, the dispute between Fluellen and Macmorris (III.ii), much of III.iii, III.iv, III.v and III.vii, a good deal of Henry's argument with his soldiers (IV.i), all of IV.iv, Burgundy's lament for France, and much

of the wooing scene (v.ii). The tradition of cuts in precisely these
areas, though nowadays by no means as extensive, still persists in
productions of the play into the 1980s. In *The Monthly Mirror* for
December 1801 it is evident that Kemble's was what Sprague
terms a 'pre-archeological production', for the reviewer complains about historical inaccuracies in Henry's throne, the Boar's
Head, the English camp at Agincourt and the modern ships and
lighthouse at Southampton. Kemble produced the play twenty-
eight times and it ran, excluding intermissions, for two hours and
forty minutes. Fifty years later Charles Kean cut about the same
number of lines, but in that age of spectacular theatre his production ran for more than four hours. Kemble was a commander
of formal demeanour in council or in battle and his royal bearing
scarcely ever gave way to a more intimate display of humanity.
One of his most famous moments was in his prayer of atonement
for Richard II when he started up at the sound of a trumpet
(Boaden, 1825, Vol. II, pp. 7–8).

Macready's productions cover the period 1815–39. At first the
Choruses were omitted but some of the lines given to other
characters. The jingoism that stirred fervour in his early productions lapsed as England and France became peaceable neighbours.
Critics complained about the battle of Agincourt in his 1837
production being fought by gentlemen in silken hose and velvet
doublets with not a single archer in view. His final appearance as
manager at Covent Garden was in his celebrated 1839 revival
which made one of the most noted textual restorations of the
century, the role of Chorus which had been omitted since 1779.
He also restored some of the cuts made by Kemble in iii.ii, iii.v,
iv.ii and iv.iii. But where Kemble had cut entirely only iii.iv
and iv.iv Macready also cut i.i, ii.i, iii.vii and iv.vi – in total 1,471
lines (43.6 per cent) in a version that ran two hours and fifty
minutes and in which he cut six characters as against the twelve
Kemble had excised. The most noted feature of the production
was Vandenhoff's Chorus in the character of Time, a russet,
bearded figure carrying scythe and hourglass, set against Stanfield's
elaborate painted illustrations. In the Prologue Time appeared on a
circular platform surrounded by clouds which then dissolved to
reveal an allegorical scene of warlike Harry with famine, sword and

fire at his heels. Dioramas were used for the other four Choruses. In the second one the conspirators were shown receiving bribes of gold from the French. In the third one the course of the English fleet to France was traced and gave place to the siege of Harfleur, an elaborate set-piece which required over a hundred performers onstage. Macready performed the role twenty times in the summer of 1839 and the tenderness and humour of his visit among the soldiers was noted. He was clearly more successful than Edmund Kean, who had, on 8 March 1830, performed the role at Drury Lane for the first and last time in the greatest fiasco of his career. *The Times* critic noted that he spoke less than a quarter of his role, either through illness or loss of memory, and was hissed throughout the first four acts. His attempt to quieten the barracking by addressing the audience before Act v drew so loud an uproar that the rest of the performance seemed to be in dumb show. One critic thought the costumes so shoddy they would have disgraced a barn.

Samuel Phelps produced the play at Sadler's Wells in 1852, 1853 and 1858. Like Macready he excised iii.iv, iii.vii and iv.iv, but unlike him presented i.i, ii.i and iv.vi. His cuts of 1,225 lines (36.3 per cent) made up a performance of two hours and forty minutes. The Chorus again appeared as Time. For iii.i there was a three-dimensional set of the fortified walls of Harfleur on which the Governor and citizens appeared. A medieval war machine, a ramp-like bridge, up which Henry led his army, was used in the assault. After the French surrender the English troops entered the city to the strains of 'The British Grenadiers'. At Agincourt Phelps used two score of actors augmented by eighty dummy figures, two strapped on to the sides of every actor, with wax heads that Madame Tussaud had manufactured (Coleman, 1886, pp. 216–17). Though the scenic effects and the accuracy of the costumes were admired, the acting itself received less praise for the weighty orations were found oppressive.

The last revival of Charles Kean at the Princess Theatre was his *Henry V* in 1859. He cut 1,460 lines (43.28 per cent) and half a dozen roles but it still lasted four hours and five minutes. He cut completely i.i, ii.i, ii.iv and iv.iv and all of iii.ii save the Boy's closing speech. Following the Act v Chorus, which was the only one to receive major cuts, he inserted a spectacular scene of Henry's triumphal return to London with the king entering on his horse beneath a tower from which angels sprinkled a shower of gold on him. A group of virgins flocked around him from the huge crowd which greeted him. Mrs Kean as Clio, the muse of history, delivered the lines of the Chorus, according to one critic, as 'an elocutionary banquet'. Tableaux were added, the three conspirators receiving bribes in Chorus II, French generals in a tent playing dice and speaking their scorn of the English (from III.vii) inserted in Chorus IV. As with Phelps, the siege of Harfleur was a scenic highlight. In his performances Kean lacked emotional subtlety but his straightforward manliness as Henry was evidently acceptable. One critic felt that during the 1850s the French were seeking any pretext to unleash an attack on an antagonist, and that this production made 'the hearts of Englishmen swell. . . . The remembrance of past heroism is a wholesome spur to national pride, a sound guarantee for the future' (Cole, 1859, p. 342). In the assault on Harfleur Kean used 212 people and his production cost over £3,000. His eighty-four performances in the role set a record. Between 1738 and 1859 there were 309 performances of the play where we know the name of the leading actor (Delane 15, Hale 8, Barry 12, Smith 56, Hull 9, Wroughton 4, Kemble 29, Elliston 2, Conway 6, Macready 28, Edmund Kean 1, Phelps 55, Charles Kean 84).

An increasingly prevailing view of Henry as a Victorian worthy was spread through the schools by Dowden's very influential primer which saw him as Shakespeare's ideal man of action. Shakespeare's text was only squeezed in between the spectacular pageants that were the main substance of the productions. Charles Calvert launched this kind of production at the Prince's Theatre in Manchester in 1872. It toured America, where it made a big impact. Rignold, in the title-role, achieved a hundred performances at the Booth theatre in 1875 and it was performed in the three following years. There was, as in Charles Kean's production, a 'Reception of Henry the Fifth entering London' with wives looking eagerly for loved ones among the returning soldiers and girls attired as angels with golden trumpets. When the production arrived at Drury Lane in 1879 the playbill asserted that 400 supernumeraries were used. The acting edition omits 1,200 lines though it seems likely more were left out. Because of the absence of significant female roles Calvert followed Kean's example and gave his wife the role of Chorus in which she appeared first as Rumour, adopted sword and shield for Harfleur, and garlands of white roses for the concluding royal wedding. The play was, no doubt, seen to have a good deal of contemporary relevance, for Bismarck had induced Napoleon to declare war on as slender a pretext as that noted in the Salic law debate. The Franco-Prussian war with its long sieges of brutal deprivation at Metz, Orléans and Paris led to a more than usual realism at Harfleur. It was clear that the jaded English army had suffered more than one repulse and were not easily driven to the breach. Much of the brutal ultimatum Henry gives to the French citizens in III.iii had been left out of productions prior to this time, and it is still severely reduced even in the productions of recent times, but Calvert, to his credit, excised only nine lines impressing the horrors of war on the audience that certainly knew how France had recently experienced them (Foulkes, 1988, p. 29). Calvert included IV.iv, severely pruned, though as a forestage scene it probably served only to allow time for the setting of the tableau for the Battle of Agincourt, just as v.i was inserted into v.ii to allow for the final setting of the cathedral at Troyes. One of the most spectacular effects of the production was the matinée idol George Rignold's entrance on stage every night on his white horse named Crispin.

The splendours of this production passed from memory and neither Henry Irving nor Beerbohm Tree attempted the role. By 1897 *The Manchester Guardian* could claim that managers avoided it because, among the historical plays, it was the one most lacking in dramatic interest. In 1897, however, Frank Benson brought it back into favour by providing many 'fine and thrilling moments' in his revival at Stratford, though some considered a dance of the two scantily attired young ladies in the French camp to be in bad taste. Between 1897 and 1916 Benson presented Henry unambiguously as the 'star of England' at Stratford sixteen times with himself in the lead all but once, Lewis Waller in 1908. Benson cut the Chorus and had a habit of pausing in his oration before Agincourt so that the sound of bells, signalling the Feast of

Crispin, might ring across the battlefield. Even when he was playing Henry in late middle age he still enjoyed his pole-vault in complete armour on to the walls at Harfleur. The fervour of patriotic spirit aroused in the Boer War brought again into vogue the presentation of the play as a recruiting poster, as *The Stratford Herald* noted in 1902:

> Even in the matter of cheery good humour and resource Harry and his handful of starved English before Agincourt seemed to share the same spirit across five centuries with Baden-Powell and the defenders of Mafeking.

But five years later the thrill had been lost and the critic was in a mood

> to remember that, after all, the whole thing – Harfleur, Agincourt ... was to little purpose ... the tide of conquest only swept back again with the arrival of Joan of Arc.

These responses perfectly catch the way the play has swung in and out of favour in response to contemporary events, anticipating how decades later, in response to Vietnam, it would be presented as an anti-war tract. The play still had a long innings as a morally uplifting epic for anglophiles. When Richard Mansfield played it in New York in 1900 he announced that he had selected the play because of

> its healthy virile tone and the lesson it teaches of honour, loyalty, courage, cheerfulness and perseverance, its beneficial influence on both old and young.

This patriotic tonic of the Boy Scout hero was certainly the effect of Lewis Waller's portrayal. When he first played the role at the Lyceum in 1900 he was 40 and was noted for grace, energy and the ringing rhetoric of his delivery. Waller apparently would lean against the furthest wall in the wings and, before his cue, push off towards door or archway so that he never just stepped on the stage but arrived full tilt. He presented, according to *The Stratford Herald*, an 'ideal man – the happy warrior, great in thought, great in purpose, great in action'. He was the star of England – almost a shooting star. When he hurtled downstage, as he built the Crispin

speech, he swung around to speak the final lines with his back to
the house and his men facing him in a semi-circle and the audience
rose to him.

It was William Poel, who directed several of the plays in the
history cycle with the Elizabethan Society, who restored the
primacy of the text. A production of *Henry V* was presented in a
lecture theatre in Burlington Gardens in 1901 and Poel also
directed a special matinée at Stratford later that year for Ben
Greet's company with an uncut text and Elizabethan staging.
Until this point the play had probably never been performed,
since Shakespeare's company had first presented it, with less than
35 per cent of the text cut. When Lewis Waller died in 1915 the
pictorial Shakespeare of the Victorians was finally being eclipsed.
With a fuller text it was possible to reveal more of the complex
variety of the play, but the 'star of England' would persist for
thirty more years. In 1920 Bridges-Adams and Robert Atkins at
the Old Vic, both followers of Poel and Granville Barker, gave the
play in almost full text and with little scenery. Bridges-Adams had
only one short interval dividing nineteen scenes, speeding up the
action with front-of-cloth scenes. Audiences used to pictorial
pageant felt robbed of their ration of grandeur while Poel thought
it 'the high-water mark of efficiency'. Both of the productions
had, as with Waller, a female Chorus. In the Old Vic performance
in 1923, with Ion Swinley in the lead, some aspects of the play had
a contemporary ring:

> The pow-wow between the two kings is like our own peace
> conferences. The soldiers are like Tommies 'fed to the teeth'
> who would so willingly have exchanged Baghdad for Bolton.
> Even the appeals to glory are our recruiting posters in better
> English. (Agate, 1943, p. 111)

Though Agate thought Ralph Richardson, in the 1931 Old Vic
production, too naturalistic and lacking in fire he did register a
newly emerging approach which was slowly to come to dominate
interpretations ('one saw the actor's intention, which was to
present Harry as a human being and not as a mailed fist, eating and
sleeping and thinking in armour' (p. 113), and he especially
commended the fearfully whispered prayer in iv.i, which had

apparently hitherto been spouted as an oration. Women continued to play the Chorus in the 1920s and 1930s, Sybil Thorndike
strutting about in a brisk performance. Gwen Frangçon Davies,
dressed as a man and very animated in a 1938 Drury Lane
production, spoke to the accompaniment of animated pictures.
Henry (Ivor Novello) and his staff at Southampton, for example,
were in a ship that moved offstage from the quayside, very much
in the Charles Kean style. Robert Atkins's 1934 production at
Stratford emphasised the spectacular in a design that had the look
of a richly ornamented medieval missal according to some, and
used costumes evidently fished out of a rag-bag according to
others. The production did nothing to dispel the commonly held
view of the play expressed by one anonymous newspaper critic:

> It has the effect upon the theatregoer of drums beating and
> bands playing. It causes an upsurging of the heart . . . but [it] is
> not a play. A pageant – yes; a procession – of course; but a play
> – never.

In explaining his approach to the role in Guthrie's 1937 Old Vic
production Olivier has written that, embarrassed by the declamatory style and influenced by the 1930s dislike of all heroism, he
tried to find ways of undercutting it. He took the Crispin speech
quietly in rehearsals until Guthrie objected that he would be
disappointing the audience by taking all the thrill out of it. He had
heard that Waller had used a side-drum roll accompaniment for
the 'breach' speech and he found that it helped. Richardson
eventually helped him by suggesting that it was impossible to play
against the text: 'I know he's a boring old scoutmaster on the face
of it, but being Shakespeare he's the exaltation of all scoutmasters.
He's the cold bath king and you have to glory in it' (Olivier, 1982,
pp. 79–80). Guthrie emphasised the pageantry by the imaginative
use of massed banners – red, blue and silver – as setting. For lovers
of the scoutmaster Henry, however, Guthrie's production, as one
might expect, was a challenge. Gordon Crosse claimed that it was
presented as 'a pacifist tract'. The Archbishop 'became an
unprincipled cleric driving a well-meaning young man into a
course which his conscience disapproved' and Crosse objected to
Olivier's display of troubled thoughtfulness because what is

needed 'is straightforward, dashing rhetoric, and no nonsense about the ethics of war' (Crosse, 1952, p. 105). Olivier was not so consciously flamboyant as he was at many points in his later film.

Iden Payne's 1937 production at Stratford, with Clement McCallin in the lead, indicated that the Bensonite legacy was not yet exhausted. Yet something of the conflict in the play was beginning to emerge for, as one critic indicated, it evoked jingoism but made you aware that it was jingoism. Some critics wondered why, if the Chorus and Henry speak so often of 'war-worn coats' among the English soldiers, the stage was all glittering armour and gay colours. But many thought that, especially in Coronation year, the pageantry was appropriate: 'It is stimulating occasionally to hang out the banners and to give ourselves a collective pat on the back' (*Birmingham Post*, 2 April 1937).

The dazzling colour and brightness was certainly one of the striking effects of Olivier's film. The colour plate illustrations of the medieval manuscript *Les Tres Riches Heures* by Pol de Limbourg and Jean Colombe, used as a basis of the set designs, gave the film an air of the romance of fairy-tales. The film was conceived in 1942, when England's fortunes were at a very low ebb, and with a clearly conscious propaganda aspect to the film. It was dedicated in its opening credits 'To the Commandos and Airborne Troops of Great Britain' and premiered on 22 November 1944, two months after the First British Airborne Division was dropped at Arnhem. Though the average film ran ninety minutes this film ran two-and-a-half hours and the colour, rarely available in the war, gave it an exotic quality. Alan Dent's original adaptation of the text cut about one-third, but eventually many scenes which were shot, such as the conspiracy scene (II.ii), were left on the cutting-room floor. Only 1,505 of 3,199 lines were used (47.04 per cent). The cuts were about half of I.ii, II.iv, III.v and III.vii, two-fifths of I.i, IV.i and V.ii, three-quarters of IV.vii, all of IV.ii and IV.iv, and virtually all of II.ii, III.iii, IV.vi and IV.viii. The tendency of these cuts has been summarised as follows:

(1) background, including both antecedent action and foreshadowing of events that follow the action; (2) much elaboration of idea, argument and detail; (3) all suggestions that England is

endangered by internal conspiracy or that Scotland is a potential threat; (4) much material involving comic characters; (5)
passages and incidents revealing Henry's character unlikely
to be attractive to modern audiences; (6) miscellaneous material
involving the French, including lines that show the French
nobles to be more spirited, worthy adversaries than the rather
weak, brash figures they are made to appear. (Geduld, 1973,
p. 48)

The result was, of course, to give a shot in the arm and a further
extended life to the noble, unblemished 'star of England', almost
saintly, one was meant to feel, from the 'halo effect' around the
king's helmet. The power and effect of this version sustains itself
for it is still shown to thousands of schoolchildren and university
students around the world each year. Henry does not condemn
Bardolph, nor threaten bloody catastrophe to the citizens of
Harfleur, nor order the execution of any French prisoners. In
the aims which it set itself the film is a powerfully successful
achievement, especially its precisely edited battle sequence which
carefully steps around all the disturbing complexities Shakespeare
sets into it. The film's most accomplished technical device is a sort
of Brechtian 'alienation effect'. The film opens on a model of
London, then settles into a very theatrical performance of Shakespeare's play in the Globe theatre and only gradually dissolves
into the 'real' world. It incorporates some of the effects of the
play's use of the Chorus in an apparent challenge of the play's
traditionalist and official ideology. Olivier's film had such a widespread effect in its portrayal of regal heroism that it may, in
large part, have prompted some later productions to find a more
complex approach by restoring to the text the passages that
Olivier, like others, omitted or to which no one had given any
emphasis for over three centuries.

The 1946 Stratford production was considered 'somnolently
static', with Paul Scofield, in the leading role, lacking in fire and
better in the quieter moments, but recognised by some as a man
probing every thought and deeper than the merely flamboyant
martial figure. One critic, noting that his sacrifice of Falstaff was 'a
chilly business', began to speculate that there might be a hint of a

darker side in the king. 'How can we feel that a man who can't be a genuine sinner could ever be a genuine saint?' The change in approaches to Henry began to accelerate when this play was presented in the context of the cycle, as it was in Stratford in 1951 and has been frequently since. It immediately produced, in Richard Burton, a Henry who was able to capitalise on the unfolding of a complex role across three plays. Many of the critics thought the heroism underplayed, for there was already in embryo some of the lonely weariness that Ian Holm and Alan Howard were to stress in the role. It was thought Burton lacked the grace and voice to fill out the patriotic epic appropriate to the Festival of Britain year. Critics found Burton too withdrawn and inward, lacking the fellow-feeling in the camp-fire talk with the soldiers. He was missing, in other words, the Chorus's version of IV.i that had hitherto always been presented instead of the high anxiety which Shakespeare shows in Henry and which Burton tried to convey, especially in the anguished appeal of his prayer. This still, often cold apartness critics had found perfectly accept-able in Burton's portrayal of Hal, but they balked when its implications were carried into the 'ideal king' for, as J. W. Lambert viewed it, Henry ought to have grown into a man 'of more tempered metal' (*Sunday Times*, 5 August 1951). The idea that Henry was still uncertain and in the process of growth baffled many critics used to him as the complete warrior. There were some, however, in 1951, like Ivor Brown in *The Observer*, who urged anyone with complaints to search the text, where they would find a great many of the elements the production emphasised. There were many more, however, who resisted this fresh approach and continued to do so when Ian Holm, Alan Howard, Kenneth Branagh and others developed it even further in the subsequent forty years. Objections to the small stature of the actors, the nasal or monotonous quality of voice insufficient to produce the ringing rhetoric, indicate that for decades critics were unwilling to accept the Henry Vs before them because they still felt cheated that they had not been offered a noble, athletic, tall, martial, uncomplicated, clarion-voiced ideal king – the figure that Lewis Waller and Olivier stamped on the first half of the century. It is fascinating to read the confusion of the critics as they bridled against versions that did not give them their lovable comic characters, the ringing orations, and the treasured moments of patriotic pride. When productions did not fill out this pattern they were said to be badly cast, disorganised and tawdry; it took a long time for critics in the press to accept that this was a deliberate approach, an assault on a sacred cow. Such an approach was difficult to accept amid the growing awareness that England's power was in precipitous decline.

Because of the mixture of Quebecois and English actors in the 1956 Stratford, Ontario production, Walter Kerr saw the play in a new light not as 'a breakneck recounting of British glories . . . [but as] a considered, ironic, delicately balanced study of national traits'. There was here the beginning of some attention to the reality of the play, for the drab, weather-worn costumes of the English were contrasted with the brilliantly colourful and rich costumes of the French. John Neville's 1960 Old Vic production featured a Mother Courage wagon which did not reconcile critics to its 'crude, tub-thumping patriotism'. The 1960 production at the Mermaid Theatre was presented in battledress and one critic thought the result incongruous:

> . . . the only recorded production in which the second half began with Chorus trying to play 'Roses of Picardy' on a mouth-organ. For that matter no Archbishop of Canterbury had ever addressed a king who wore cricket flannels, and who was clearly straight from the field. The night scene, 'an essay in war', with battle noises in full volume was less like *Henry V* than a close study of modern warfare with Shakespearian illustrations. (Trewin, 1964, p. 231)

The irony Gerald Gould saw in the play in 1919 was beginning to dominate productions in part, no doubt, because of the impact Brecht, reinforced by the visit of the Berliner Ensemble, was having on English theatre. In reporting on German productions in 1964 Kenneth Tynan indicated how radical productions there could be. A performance in Bremen, ironically retitled *Henry Hero*, was performed in First World War costumes with the king as a cynical, bullet-headed thug who delivered the exhortation on the eve of Agincourt not to his generals but to a French whore with whom he was in bed. In III.vii the French leaders sipped wine around a Christmas tree beside which an English prisoner was being tortured. To ensure that the audience made no mistake in its attitude to Henry there was a backcloth adorned with painted heads of leaders from Attila the Hun to Elvis Presley (Tynan, 1967, p. 154).

In the 1964 RSC production Ian Holm was very much a democratic Henry, scarcely distinguishable in costume from his men. His speech before Harfleur was more a desperate plea than a rallying cry. Some critics began to see the play as something much better than its reputation:

> The only relic of what might be the Olivier–Elgar approach, a trumpet voluntary to the pomp and circumstance of glorious war, is to be found in the grandiloquent mouthings of the Chorus. (Alan Brien, *Sunday Telegraph*, 7 June 1964)

J. R. Brown objected that the Chorus was allowed to make flourishes about a quite different play, as if the directors believed that all he said was ironically wrong. A glance at the programme would have confirmed that that was precisely the director's view: '. . . the play is a criticism of the Chorus's view of the story'. In his notes in the programme Peter Hall indicated that here was a production which responded to some of the complexity of the play:

> Henry V is empirically great, not always morally great. If you have to be a king and do your job you become a pattern of contradictions. Henry is, therefore, both a devious politician and a man of sincerity; a hypocrite and an idealist. The Church's role . . . is totally political. Henry's prayers are, like most things about him, ambiguous. . . . [The play] is a celebration of war and a criticism of war. An ambiguous document: Shakespeare usually is.

This questioning approach was very evident in Michael Langham's 1966 Stratford, Ontario production. As the king, Douglas Rain exhibited ostentatious piety and was a hard man always on the verge of failure, shouldering his burden of kingship with reluctance, a plodding man so troubled by growing worries as to move almost into paranoid isolation. He wooed his princess very bluntly as a matter of policy and statecraft. Despite its reputation for glorifying war Langham indicated, in his programme notes, that the play was shot through with disillusion with the inanities of nationalism. The Chorus, he believed, represents the popular view, the national press, 'Time' and 'Life' against which the detail of the play must be made to work. Towards that end he had the troops strip the dead of spoils, listen blank-eyed and indifferent to Henry's pep talks, and jeer his pious dedications of victory to God. This tendency was developed to an even greater extreme in Michael Kahn's 1969 production at Stratford, Connecticut. Kahn told one interviewer he thought it 'obscene' to do the play as a straight nationalistic epic. He thought Henry a man full of contradictions and that the play indicates that there are no 'heroes' without blood on their hands. The production unfolded amid the swings and climbing bars of a playground setting to emphasise the idea that the play is about games of war, power, betrayal and love. Most critics found it a crude anti-war tract and a cheapening of the play. The Brechtian devices of using titles to announce segments of the action, such as Scene 7, 'Siege of Harfleur, Propaganda of the Machine; The People Follow', worked all too effectively in alienating the audience. It was becoming evident in several productions that the balance which had been ignored for centuries by the emphasis on one side was now being replaced by an emphasis on the other. The simple-minded patriotic hymn was becoming the simple-minded anti-war tract. Critics strove to retain some sense of the balance of the play:

> . . . there is no question of a hysterically adverse view of Henry and the invasion. It is, rather, a matter of bringing the darker, more sceptical passages into a living relation with the heroically straightforward. (Berry, 1981, p. 67)

The Terry Hands RSC 1975 production, with Alan Howard in the lead, tried hard to get some effective balance in the play, though it still failed to convey the full range of which it is capable. There was no attempt to present a glamorous, heroic contest, nor was it a satirical account of the bloodthirsty brutalities of war. Throughout the Henriad, Howard was striving to come to terms with kingship. Though he was just hard enough to take the necessary, ruthless decisions he was not a natural soldier and was often wracked by anguish and emotional conflict. As Ronald Bryden phrased it in the programme:

> The education Shakespeare imagines for his hero is an actor's education: the rehearsal of an infinite variety of roles in preparation for the greatest role of all.

This was reinforced in the programme notes with pages of quotations on role-playing from various figures such as St Augustine, Erving Goffman, Garrick, Sartre and Beckett. Howard never let the audience forget that he was approaching his task with great circumspection and it was exacting a great cost. Terry Hands was critical of the cuts Olivier had made and did not believe his film was a reflection of the play Shakespeare wrote. He called the RSC 1964 production the Vietnam anti-war version. He considered the play to be less about war than about Henry V, about a man learning to know his people and the task of governing them, a necessary task resulting from the occupation in which his father had knocked away a lot of the divinity that hedges a king so that the role and the person were no longer one. The result, as one critic viewed it, was that Hands was able to consider, with Shakespeare, what it is that we require from heroes. Another critic felt that the production embraced the principle that where history records what men did, drama records what they felt while they were doing it. The aspect of the production which provoked most discussion was the decision to open the play with the actors in casual, modern rehearsal clothes, transferring to period costume only when the play was well launched. It was an attempt to achieve a somewhat similar effect to Olivier's use of the framing device of the Globe theatre performance. Hands started with the idea that rehearsal is a period of experimental communication to emphasise the view that Henry is constantly exploring and trying out provisional roles which regenerate the next stage of his character. The device, however, confused many audiences. More successful was the single canopy Farrah designed for the play. Above the heads of the actors it was brilliantly heraldic, echoing the varied colours of rhetoric and battle glory in the play. Dropped to the stage it became an irregular dull terrain, the bleak reality of a wearying war, so that this one scenic effect vividly enfolded within itself the contradictory elements shot through the play. By judicious cutting, however, this production managed to avoid some of the harsher realities of the war. Those harsh realities were very much the focus of Michael Bogdanov's production (ESC, 1986). The atmosphere was clearly modelled after the decadent, on-the-skid England of the 1980s. Michael Pennington's king was a cold, conniving unappealing Tory patronising a rag-tag army of public school chaps barely in control of a lower order of yobs and petty crooks. The meanness, violence and visceral rapacity were not at all concealed by a civilised veneer in a society where ideals were merely exploitable strategies to gain an edge in a world of brutish inequality.

In the 1984 RSC production the director, Adrian Noble, thought the recent Falkland's campaign made the grisly reality of war and the hysteria that promoted it newly relevant. Several critics felt that the emphasis on violence, barely suppressed in Kenneth Branagh's reading of Henry, and culminating in the garrotting on stage of Bardolph, was done at the expense of other elements in the play. After Agincourt corpses lay in ghastly rows across the stage and some felt that the aim of the production was to achieve the complete opposite of Olivier's heroic tone. Henry was played very much as an emotionally strained figure. He collapsed into tears of anguish or relief on key occasions to indicate that his youth had been tried almost beyond its strength. Even the Chorus was played with a sceptical cynicism, aware that the promotion of patriotism was a kind of transparent puffery. The misery of the Picardy campaign was constantly emphasised in the drab, worn uniforms of the English who huddled together under tarpaulin sheets as the rain pelted down. Branagh responded to the countercurrents in the role and believed firmly that his piety and humility were genuine but that the violent threats before Harfleur could only come from 'a professional killer of chilling ruthless-ness' so that it would be 'ridiculous to play him as a one-dimensional Machiavel' (Jackson and Smallwood, 1988, pp. 97–100). But the idea still persisted among critics that the attempted complexity was imposed by a clever young director and not in the play itself. These phrases are culled from many reviews: 'this rabble rousing play', 'this long, blustering play that so glorifies war', 'Shakespeare's version of "There'll always be an England"', 'the most obviously patriotic of Shakespeare's plays'. There are evidently many who still feel that Henry is an unambiguous hero, others who feel that Shakespeare's version of Henry is a white-wash job that is out of tune with our times, still others who feel that left-wing RSC directors are doing a demolition job on Shakespeare's straightforward play. Directors sensitive to these different strands of resistance often try hard, as Gareth Lloyd Evans suggested, to reconcile two contradictory approaches, the modish modern view that the play is an embarrassing reminder of England's jingoistic and disgustingly Imperial past and the view that it is a worthy celebration of Great Britishness, with the result, as Evans phrased it, that Noble 'seems both to take the mickey and blow the trumpet' (*Stratford-Upon-Avon Herald*, 6 April 1984), trying to achieve an impossible mixture of naturalism and ritual. Noble did not get the countercurrents into an effective balance, but in recognising that they are irreconcilable he did touch on the play's power to disturb members of an audience by forcing them to confront irreconcilable elements in themselves.

Branagh in his 1989 film is unable to improve on Noble's flawed grasp of the dynamics of the play. Branagh's Henry is a tougher nut than in Noble's production, gritty, hard-nosed, colder, not quite as much the young warrior being tempered in the fire of war, and sacrificing more of his humanity in pursuing his war. The drab décor is augmented by the claustrophobic airlessness of studio sets. The limited budget and the excessive use of close-ups produces a TV rather than a film quality, very much in the constricted style of the BBC Shakespeare series. Every attempt is made to avoid the colourful fairy-tale quality of the Olivier film. In the muddy campaign life is grubby, brutish and short. One of the most prominent events is an incident not in Shakespeare's onstage action, the hanging of Bardolph. The battle of Agincourt is as great a contrast as possible to Olivier's archers and his cavalry charge across a sunlit plain. It is something of a poor man's *Ran* (Kurosawa's *Lear*), with an emphasis on mud and the chaotic waste of war in its struggle of crazed figures. Branagh cuts as much of the text as Olivier, much of it in exchange for this dance of death, which, in twenty minutes, is not even remotely as effective as the definitive portrait of war's madness in less than half the time in Orson Welles's account of Shrewsbury in *Chimes at Midnight*.

John Wood's production at Stratford, Ontario in 1989 also placed heavy emphasis on the brutality of the war, the onstage slitting of the French prisoners' throats and the brutal slaying of the Boy being prominent features. Like the 1960s production at the Mermaid Theatre the play was transposed to the First World War, incorporating a recruiting concert party with Gilbert and Sullivan songs and ditties of the 1914 period. This production captured more effectively than any modern production what one critic defines as the qualities of the first two acts, the initial surge of enthusiasm and 'the holiday atmosphere of the first days of a military campaign when the true face of war is hidden behind the waving banners' (Ornstein, 1972, p. 180). Henry was not presented as a devious, role-playing strategist but as a dashing, blond, public school figure. A somewhat naive, eager house-captain looking for a 'good war', he found his men to be a mixture of 'decent types' and seedy scoundrels. As he discovered that he had bitten off a good deal more than he could chew, the war became a very sobering experience in which he was hard pressed to retain the stiffness of his upper lip. His role-playing was very much a modern aristocrat's determination not to lose face before his men. The pursuit of honour and glory was a preoccupation only of the class-privileged and eccentrics like Fluellen. The British tommies fought reluctantly and only responded to patriotic fervour when it could help them to control their terror. Many audiences and several critics were unable to recognise that the play was questioning heroism and still felt that the production had failed to reflect the promotion of battle glory which they were convinced was Shakespeare's principal intention in the play.

A number of persistent traditions have become associated with productions of the play. In the Branagh film and the 1989 Stratford, Ontario production the Prelates featured in the first two scenes are clearly skilled, manipulative politicians. This is a new tradition of the last few decades which replaces an older one of very long standing, and which reached its peak in Olivier's film, that they are bumbling fools. For well over a century Charles VI

was played as a figure sunk in extreme senility, as in Harcourt
Williams's performance in Olivier's film. Holinshed mentions
madness in the historical French king but there is no evidence in
the play that Shakespeare used the idea. In Benson's productions
he was often a crafty old dotard whose attention was divided
between affairs of state and a Fool who amused him with cards and
a cup-and-ball. Waller produced a similar figure who had intervals
of vigorous sanity (Crosse, 1952, p. 44). Victorian productions
often presented dancing girls in the French camp, Isadora Duncan
once taking such a role, to emphasise a Gallic looseness of morals.
The Chorus from the 1850s to the 1940s was often played by a
woman, sometimes like Sybil Thorndike as a page, sometimes as
the Muse of History or Time. Poel's presentation of the role as an
Elizabethan student was thought revolutionary because it had
been played by a woman for so long. The role of Pistol was
obviously a theatre draw from the outset for he is mentioned in the
title of the 1600 Quarto. Theopilus Cibber specialised in the role
from 1740 onwards and succeeded, according to an account of
the time, 'by a laughable importance of deportment, extrava-
gant grimaces and . . . speaking it in the sonorous cant of old
tragedians' – a style that persists to this day, as so often also does
Cibber's use of a ridiculously large hat. In most of the productions
prior to the turn of this century, and in more than half of the
productions after it, he has been deprived of his scene with Le Fer.
The resemblances between the Dauphin and Cloten are reinforced
in many productions. It used to be common for a terrified peasant
girl to be seen escaping his lust, or to provide him with a mistress to slap around. Even though the character of Henry has
undergone radical reinterpretation in the last four decades these
traditional stereotypes associated with the play have often persisted, which is testimony to the deep conservatism of many
theatrical habits, and helps also to explain why there has often
been resistance to, or confusion in face of, such re-evaluations.

# Critical Reception

For some the play presents the story of an ideal monarch and glorifies his achievements; for them the tone approaches that of an epic lauding the military virtues. For others the protagonist is a Machiavellian militarist who professes Christianity but whose deeds reveal both hypocrisy and ruthlessness; for them the tone is predominantly one of mordant satire. (Wentersdorf, 1976, p. 265)

For two centuries many of the most distinguished critics from Dr Johnson to Dover Wilson have disagreed about the nature of Henry V. Making a virtue of necessity some recent critics have argued that contradictory versions are inscribed in the text of the play and reflect a division within Shakespeare's own mind. The majority of critics, however, have insisted that Henry is either a golden hero or a ruthless thug. Many of the partisans of both sides have agreed that the quality of the play is inferior. A glance through Michael Quinn's useful collection (1969) of critical views of the play provides a range of negative responses (page reference in parentheses after each extract).

[Dr Johnson] The truth is, that the poet's matter failed him in the fifth act, and he was glad to fill it up with whatever he could get; and not even Shakespeare can write well without a proper subject. (p. 33)

[Thomas Kenny] ... the work on the whole is forcible, eloquent, and declamatory, rather than vital, passionate, and dramatic. (p. 42)

[Sidney Lee] *Henry V* is as far as possible from what is generally understood by a drama. It is without intrigue or entanglement; it propounds no problems of psychology, its definite motive is neither comic nor tragic; women play in it the slenderest part; it lacks any plot in the customary sense. (p. 56)

[Masefield] It is a chronicle or procession eked out with soldiers' squabbles . . . [Henry is] the one commonplace man in eight plays. (pp. 61–2)

[Mark Van Doren] . . . the style of *Henry V* [is] fatty rather than full, relaxed instead of restrung. (p. 119)

[J. I. M. Stewart] Falstaff's corner of *Henry V* is extremely wonderful; the rest is a slack-water play, stirred here and there by simple patriotic feeling. (p. 72)

[Peter Alexander] . . . a thing of shreds and patches, held together by the Choruses . . . not so much a play as a pageant. (p. 128)

Critics unable to find the thread which unites its elements constantly bring expectations to the play they claim it does not fulfil. Many judgements on the confused, uneven texture of the play stem from the eighteenth-century view that comic sequences in the play are no more than coarse, episodic ornament inserted for the pleasure of the groundlings. Once they are seen as an integral part of the argument, one of the elements in a dialectical relation with the version of events of the Chorus, the attitudes of the French, and Henry's struggle to sustain his campaign, then the play works on stage, on the rare occasions when it is not savagely cut, as a complex examination of war from a carefully organised variety of perspectives.

The carping of critics notwithstanding, the play on stage, in-variably edited until recently into a heroic pageant, has been a sure-fire draw that could be relied on to produce throbbing hearts and swelling breasts in an audience of patriots. In the most recent productions, which present something more, though rarely all, of its full complexity, it has been discovered to share a quality of all the history plays. Once thought to be ill-constructed and episodic, they are now discovered to make an audience oscillate throughout between attraction to and repulsion from the central characters. Such an oscillation is inescapable in our responses to Richard II, Bolingbroke, Falstaff, Hotspur and Hal in the earlier plays in this tetralogy. It is becoming possible to see that 'little in [*Henry V*] is perfunctory or indifferent. . . . The poetry is always more than adequate to its dramatic purpose' (Ornstein, 1972, p. 175).

Those who accept Henry unambiguously as 'the star of England' have no interest in or recognition of the complex countercurrents of the play. Henry has been described as:

> . . . the spiritual wholesome type. (Lee, 1906, p. 175)

> . . . the Messiah of true kingliness. He is both wholly respon-
> sive to the divine responsibility he holds and also wholly
> glorified by temporal success. (Knight, 1958, p. 37)

> . . . a eulogistic portrait of a conquering hero. (Ribner, 1957,
> p. 183)

Typical of this approach is John Dover Wilson's dedication of his New Cambridge edition to Viscount Wavell, 'Star of England' in her darkest night, from whose *Life of Allenby* he claimed to have learned more about Henry than from all the critics put together, a king who deserved the homage and affection owing to a Nelson or a Gordon. He related the play in 1947, as so many previous productions had done, to contemporary events:

> The war against France is a righteous war; and seemed as much
> so to Shakespeare's public as war against the Nazis seems to us.
> Once this is realized a fog of suspicion and detraction is lifted
> from the play; the mirror held up in 1599 shines bright once
> more and we are at liberty to find a hero's face reflected within
> it. (Wilson, 1947, p. xxiv)

He believed that Henry's words before Agincourt and Churchill's after the Battle of Britain come from 'the same national mint' (xxxi). Others have agreed, though not always with such eager approval, that it is

> a propaganda play on National Unity: heavily orchestrated for the brass. . . . The wartime values demand a determined 'one-eyedness' (Rossiter, 1961, pp. 57–8)

Modern critics, eager to defend Henry against his detractors, indicate that virtually all of Shakespeare's contemporaries saw him as an entirely admirable king, often listed among the great heroes of the past such as King Arthur, Alexander, the Black Prince:

> . . . as near as makes no matter he is made to embody the classical and Renaissance conceptions of the ideal king, ideals which coincide with the uncommon nobility yet the essential humanity of the epic hero. . . . To see a deep irony on Shakespeare's part, a deep ambiguity about the figure of Henry, is fatally to misread what its first audience must have seen. (Moseley, 1988, p. 98)

We are advised by E. E. Stoll not to import modern sensibilities in evaluating past events:

> Some readers may object a little to Henry's obtrusive morality and his familiarity with the Most High. They may be reminded of later czars and kaisers, likewise engaged in wars of aggression, and be inclined to call it hypocrisy or official cant. Shakespeare surely did not mean it so; the Elizabethans would not have taken it so. (Berman, 1968, p. 101)

As Henry's reputation began to come under increasing assault in this century a stern rearguard action was conducted by J. H. Walter in his influential Arden edition, in which he argued that Henry fits the precepts of the model prince outlined by Erasmus.

Those who have, to use the language of Walter, 'calumniated' Henry in a way that is 'destructive of the moral epic purpose of the play' (Walter, 1954, p. xxii) have been at the task a long time, as extracts from Quinn's collection reveal:

> [Hazlitt] Henry V . . . in public affairs seemed to have no idea of any rule of right or wrong, but brute force glossed over with

a little religious hypocrisy and archiepiscopal advice. (Quinn, 1969, p. 36)

[Yeats] He has the gross vices, the coarse nerves, of one who is to rule among violent people, and he is so little 'too friendly' to his friends that he bundles them out of doors when their time is over. He is as remorseless and undistinguished as some natural force. . . . (p. 55)

The recoil from the barbarous sacrifices of the First World War were sufficient explanations to some for resistance to the play. J. W. Cunliffe (1916, pp. 320–1) indicated that we no longer believe in Divine Right, are suspicious of religiosity and rhetoric and so naturally do not yield up the unqualified admiration common in earlier periods. Gould argued that precisely because Shakespeare was patriotic he must have been revolted by Henry's brutal and degrading militarism and that the play is 'a satire on monarchical government, on imperialism, on the baser kinds of "patriotism", and on war' (Quinn, 1969, p. 83). Hobday (1968, p. 109) is convinced that Shakespeare must have regarded Henry as a murderer since he 'constantly juxtaposed the fine talk of honour and religion with the realities of human greed and cruelty'. The prevailing tendency in recoiling from Henry as a manipulative Machiavel has been to emphasise a cold, inhuman efficiency which the bluff persona inadequately conceals, a quality most effectively summed up by Una Ellis Fermor:

He has inured himself so steadfastly to the life of a king, lived so long in councils and committees, weighing, sifting, deciding, commanding, that his brain automatically delivers a public speech where another man utters a cry of despair, of weariness or of prayer . . . and only when we try to look into the heart of the man do we find . . . that the character has been converted whole to the uses of his function, the individual utterly eliminated, sublimated if you will. There is no Henry, only a king. . . . For the truth is that Shakespeare himself, now that he has built the figure with such care, out of the cumulative experience of eight plays, begins to recoil from it. (Quinn, pp. 128–30)

In the face of these polarised opinions about Henry and his play
we can choose pro or contra or we can believe that Shakespeare
could not make up his mind and left confusion. Or we can take one
strand of evidence to represent Shakespeare's intentional meaning while acknowledging that he cannot help but include other
evidence because he cannot fully believe what he is trying to say.
There are issues throughout the play which have caused critics to
leap to its defence or to indict its hero: the warmongering plotting
of the prelates at the outset to safeguard their own property,
Henry's trapping of the conspirators, his savage threats to compel
submission at Harfleur, his hanging of Bardolph, his prayer before
battle, his order to slit the French prisoners' throats, his lack of
interest in the fate of ordinary soldiers killed in battle. Many of
these details, most of which are Shakespeare's elaboration of his
sources, need not have been presented at all or not in a manner
which unsettles the audience. Several critics and a few productions
insist that there is in Henry 'an uneasy balance between unbridled
passion and cold self-control' (Traversi, 1957, p. 172). This suggests that the contradictions are placed quite deliberately in the
play:

> Shakespeare creates a work whose ultimate power is precisely
> the fact that it points in two opposite directions, virtually
> daring us to choose one of the two opposed interpretations it
> requires of us. (Rabkin, 1977, p. 279)

> Shakespeare seems to have decided that . . . he would prepare
> an overt text and a secret play in parallel – the one would be for
> the jingoes and the common informers: the other for people
> who thought as he did but could not safely say so. (Arden,
> 1977, p. 199)

There are, however, comparatively few such critics who are
willing to accept that the ultimate effectiveness of the play depends
on the tension that is produced when we find ourselves accepting
both views of Henry, sometimes alternately, but often simultaneously. Shakespeare, at a critical point in history, was way ahead
of his time in coming to terms with the inevitable drift in political
behaviour. He faces the unpalatable 'truth', out of the long and

vexed history of England recorded in his cycle of plays, that a leader must sustain the impression that he is strong, secure, wise and just even while unscrupulously pursuing the means that will ensure his success. Such a figure, it has been suggested, was a result of change in the sixteenth century from horror at Machiavellian tactics to an acceptance of them, in a somewhat tamed form, as a necessary skill in successful government, so that in:

> keeping such a monarch attractive to his audience despite what they might know or suspect about his methods, Shakespeare was creating a model for most Western political leaders to follow – be they kings, prime ministers or presidents. (Manheim, 1973, p. 4)

Terry Hands, who directed a successful recent production (SE, 1975), believes the play speaks directly to many of our modern uncertainties about politics, which makes critical resistance to its qualities the more amazing:

> I really cannot see how the play has earned its unflattering epithets. There is enough in it to satisfy every pacifist, warrior, poet, peasant, scientist and sectarian. . . . And yet perversely the superb text is ignored – the contradictions, the complexities, the sheer Shakespearianness of it all – and Shakespeare in full control of his powers at that. (Beauman, 1976, p. 21)

This play, as critics are gradually coming to understand, though long regarded as a simple-minded pageant or a confused failure, is one of the most underrated plays in the canon, inescapably controversial, and containing a complex multiplicity which recent productions have only begun to explore.

# The Text

The heroic version of the play which held the stage for so long was produced not simply by the décor and the acting but by the radical editing of the text which, before this century, usually eliminated 35–45 per cent of the play. The cutting in this century has been less radical but, more often than not, almost as effective in distorting the balance of elements in the play. It is worth noting that of the productions at the various Stratfords Iden Payne's 1937 production in England is the only one that cut less than 16 per cent of the text, and even he came almost 300 lines short of Poel's production, the only one I can find which claimed to be uncut. Iden Payne's production was one of the last examples of a presentation of the play without transpositions or a redistribution of the lines of the Chorus, following the order of most modern texts, as increasingly few productions do. I will comment on specific effects of cutting in my analysis of the play, but I register here the size of the cuts in a number of significant productions of the last sixty years. Stratford, England: 1934 (22.6%), 1937 (8.5%), 1943 (40.7%) (probably affected by wartime conditions), 1946 (18.3%), 1951 (17.3%), 1964 (23.1%), 1971 (31.0%) (a Theatregoround production more heavily cut for touring), 1975 (16.6%), 1984 (17.8%); Stratford, Ontario: 1956 (17.5%), 1966 (19.2%), 1980 (24.9%); ESC 1986 (19.4%). The Olivier film cut nearly 53 per cent, the Branagh film of 1989 cut 53.5 per cent, the 1979 BBC TV version cut 15.9 per cent. It is useful to remember the caution Berners Jackson issued in *The Hamilton Spectator* in his review of a severely filleted production (SO, 1966):

> It is conceivable that those who did the cutting and hacking can write a better play than Shakespeare could. It is even conceivable that they could write a better play about Henry V – doubtful but conceivable. But what they cannot do is write a better Shakespeare play than Shakespeare did.

The text of this play, compared to that of many of Shakespeare's others, is not problematic. What is generally agreed to be a 'bad quarto' was published in 1600 (Q1), and was reprinted, with minor corrections, in 1602 (Q2) and 1619 (Q3). Q leaves out the Choruses, omits 1.i, 111.i and 1v.ii and has evidently been cut to provide a script suitable for provincial performances with a considerably reduced cast of eleven. It is considered by some scholars to be a memorially reconstructed text stemming probably from the player of Gower and/or Exeter. The Folio text has been printed, most scholars agree, on the evidence of the erratic stage directions, from Shakespeare's 'foul papers'. It may represent the text before it was prepared for the theatre by the Company's prompter. It has been argued, by Gary Taylor (1979, 1982), that Q is derived from a textual source representing a later stage in the play's development than the Folio text does, and may contain certain changes made by Shakespeare himself when transcribing the foul papers on which F is evidently based, or as a result of suggestions made in rehearsal and production. For Taylor, in his Oxford edition, this gives Q, at times, an authority which F lacks. In this view the availability of no more than eleven actors explains virtually every major anomaly in Q's distribution of scenes and characters, the omission of 111.i and 1v.ii, the transposition of 1v.iv and 1v.v and the omission of the Chorus (Wells and Taylor, 1979, p. 72). Taylor points out (1982, p. 12) that some of these omissions are elements which seem to cast a questionable emphasis on Henry's achievements: 1.i and 1.ii.115–35, which indicates the Church's financial support for the war; references in 11.i to Henry's responsibility for Falstaff's sickness; the hint by Cambridge in 11.ii.154–9 of dynastic motives for his conspiracy which touch on Henry's shaky claim to the throne; the character of Macmorris and much of Henry's ruthless threats at Harfleur in iii.iii; and Burgundy's description of a ravaged France in v.ii.38–62. Another critic has disputed Taylor's view that the quarto was abridged for a company travelling outside London and the more general view that it is a 'bad' quarto memorially reconstructed. Patterson believes that the quarto abridgement may have resulted from a need to avoid entanglement in the problems of Essex, trouble which the Folio version, and especially the topical reference to him in Chorus v, could have brought on the company. For authorities highly sensitive to the slightest questioning of regal authority it was prudent to produce 'an *almost* unproblematic view of a highly popular monarch whose most obvious analogy was Elizabeth herself' (Patterson, 1988, p. 46). She believes that

> the abridgement was a tactical retreat from one kind of play to another, from a complex historiography that might have been misunderstood to a symbolic enactment of nationalist fervour. (Patterson, p. 41)

For centuries patriots resistant to the complexity of the play have striven on stage to edit it into a simple heroic account. Patterson suggests that the first to undertake such a task to avoid political trouble may have been Shakespeare himself. The quarto version certainly does edit out much material that is unflattering to Henry. What this theory does not explain is why it also leaves out the Choruses which are the chief exhibits of the patriotic fervour Patterson argues the quarto is designed to promote. Whatever the origin of the quarto it is clear that it is the Folio which presents Shakespeare working at full stretch.

# Prologue: 'You are too much mistaken in this king': Henry in the tetralogy

We have come to accept that the real strength and originality of Shakespeare's drama lies in its multiple unity based on contrasts in its array of plots and characters. These ensure that the issues raised are constantly seen in shifting lights as though through the different facets of a crystal. John Lyly, as a classically trained author, looked on this developing stockpot of dramatic form with some anxiety but aware that it was an irresistible trend:

> Time hath confounded our mindes, our mindes the matter; but all cometh to this passe, that what heretofore hath been served in several dishes for a feaste, is now minced in a charger for a Gallimaufrey. If we presente a mingle-mangle our fault is to be excused because the whole worlde is become a Hodge-podge.
> (Bond, 1902, Vol. 3, p. 115)

The first recorded use of 'gallimaufrey' to mean a heterogeneous mass of elements is in More's *Utopia* (1551–6) in connection with drama, 'such a tragycall comedye or gallimaufreye'. It would not be long before Polonius would list his amazing medley of dramatic forms (*Hamlet*, ii.ii.392–7). The text of *Henry V*, like his others, demonstrates Shakepeare's view of life as a mingle-mangle or, in the words of the Second Lord in *All's Well That Ends Well*:

> The web of our life is of a mingled yarn, good and ill together.
> Our virtues would be proud if our faults whipt them not; and
> our crimes would despair if they were not cherished by our
> virtues. (IV.iii.67–70)

Of this mingled yarn *Henry V* is, in my view, one of Shakespeare's
principal examples. Only if we accept in analysis and put on stage
all of the strands of the text, what Polonius calls 'scene individ-
able', can we understand its power as a single play and its full effect
in the tetralogy of which it is the culminating part. The nature of
that mingled yarn becomes clear when we recognise the modifica-
tions Shakespeare made to the chronicle accounts that he used to
enliven the French campaign.

Specific details of Henry's reign were passed down by popular
tradition to establish a myth about him which Shakespeare found
ready made: (a) the wildness of his youth and his complete
conversion to piety on his accession; (b) the gift of the tennis balls
from the Dauphin and his reply; (c) the man executed as an
example, for theft from a church, during the French campaign;
(d) his speech before Agincourt prompted by one of his com-
manders' wishes for more men. To a degree Shakespeare was
bound by these traditions but he was free to give them a framing of
his own choosing to throw a new light on the myth. Henry's
conquest of France was in three stages: (1) in 1415 he took
Harfleur and achieved victory at Agincourt; (2) a sustained campaign from 1417–20 to control Normandy concluded by the
Treaty of Troyes; (3) a series of sieges in 1421–2 which ended with
Henry's death. By telescoping these varied phases over seven
years into one seemingly lightning drive to triumph Shakespeare
might appear to be, like his Chorus, polishing up the image of
Henry's miraculously heroic success. Shakespeare clearly did not
think that the Chorus, drawing only on events in the chronicles,
gave a complete account of the campaign. In range and variety
Shakespeare went far beyond the crude clowning available in the
source play. *The Famous Victories of Henry the Fifth* is, according
to one critic, 'about as subtle as a meat cleaver and is jingoistic
centuries before the idea was invented' (Moseley, 1988, p. 76).
This play was registered for publication on 14 May 1594, though

probably performed, with Tarleton in the role of Dericke, the clown, well before that date. The unique and heavily abridged text which survives was published in 1598 by Thomas Creede. The details which Shakespeare adapted from a play that seem very much like a 'modern strip-cartoon' (Tydeman, 1987, p. 43) were all transmuted to fit into his complex account of the conquest. There is no doubt, given the popularity of Henry V, that one of the chief factors Shakespeare had to deal with when he came to write his play was the audience's expectations about this king's most famous victories. Whether to go along with that tradition, radically modify it, or subtly challenge it, would be a prime consideration for a dramatist who had developed such skills in seeing all sides of an issue and in exploiting ambiguity in language, character and plot. We can see how much Shakespeare made the story his own by noting the material that is predominantly his own invention or an ingenious elaboration of material far beyond the resources of the crude clowning of *The Famous Victories*: II.i, II.iii , III.ii, III.iv, III.vi.1–109, III.vii, IV.i.35–301, IV.iv, IV.vii.11–51, 114–78, IV.viii.1–70, 115–19 , V.i, V.ii. 99–277. The material he invented to augment and enliven the historical actions recounted in his chronicle sources totals 1,430 lines, or 44.4 per cent of the play.

In the whole play there are forty-three named figures in the dramatis personae and twenty-nine of these are figures that could have been featured, or at least mentioned, in the chronicles. There are, however, a baker's dozen of characters, nearly a third, who could not be found there. Such commoners in the list of the battle dead (IV.viii.100–3) would be dismissed in the phrase 'none else of name'. In Shakespeare's play they are by no means anonymous – Gower, Fluellen, Macmorris, Jamy, Bates, Court, Williams, Nym, Bardolph, Pistol, Boy, Nell Quickly, Le Fer. They have a number of scenes to themselves and a prominent role in several others. Perhaps most impressive is the fact that six of them have important contributions in the scene that is the climactic turning-point of the play (IV.i). We can see their significance in the way that the spoken lines are distributed in the play: Henry speaks 31.1%, the Chorus 6.9%, the English and French nobility (28 characters) 35.8%, the thirteen commoners Shakespeare uses to augment his sources

26.2%. If we include also the interactions the king has with his commoners we find that their concerns contribute 976 lines to the play, over 30% of it (II.i, II.iii, III.ii, III.vi.1–109, IV.i.35–225, IV.iv, IV.vii.1–51, 89–111, 115–64, IV.viii.1–70, v.i). Shakespeare is not here simply following the pattern of *The Famous Victories* or of the two previous plays in this tetralogy, for none of those plays has a Chorus persistently promoting a version of events which is much less complex than the one we actually experience. Shakespeare is often faithful to his sources but he adopts an interrogative approach to them. He edits out certain elements, expands others and, by adding characters of his own invention, alters the proportions of the constituent elements and thereby puts his stamp on the story. In so many of his plays he seems to be saying to his audience 'I realise you think you know this story but let us see what really happened'. For a long time critics and productions exempted *Henry V* from this pattern. The difference between the productions of the eighteenth and nineteenth century and the recent ones can be easily explained. Of the 976 lines cited above relating to the commoners' concerns productions before this century cut as much as 45 per cent. The modern production that emphasised most clearly the very mixed nature of Henry's army, Michael Bogdanov's (ESC, 1986), cut 2 per cent of those lines. It is worth noting that Branagh's film, widely celebrated for moderating the picture of the heroic Henry with a realistic depiction of war's horrors, nevertheless cut 63 per cent of these lines. The Chorus proposes a very English play, one the audience might have expected, from 'the brightest heaven of invention'. Shakespeare, however, provides a climate that is even more English – variable cloudiness with sunny intervals and occasional showers.

There are critics who have seen Shakespeare's second tetralogy of history plays as being organised to illustrate the morality and training of a Prince to produce an ideal king. Sherman Hawkins sees the *Henry IV* plays as organised around four cardinal virtues – temperance and fortitude in Part 1, justice and wisdom in Part 2, which shows how a good man is first made lord of himself and then ruler of the state. He finds it impossible to believe that Shakespeare trained his student prince in all of these virtues only to make him out, as others have claimed, a prig and a hypocrite dehumanised by his kingly role. Walter, in the Arden edition, argues that Henry fits the model of the ideal prince as laid down in Erasmus' *Institutio Principis Christiani* of 1516 possessed of all 'the king becoming graces'. As others have pointed out, however, Erasmus strongly insists that a prince must avoid any trumped-up pretext for military adventure because war is the worst misfortune that can befall a people, a point forcibly made by some of Henry's soldiers in iv.i. Erasmus urges princes to seek the advice of clerics who should attempt to deflect and dissuade arguments for war, which is precisely the opposite of what happens in the first two scenes of Shakespeare's play. Henry's threats at Harfleur in trying to achieve military success are very far from the Erasmian model. Various writers have asserted that the interpretation of the character of Henry V can easily be settled by acceptance of the idea that Shakespeare was a captive of providential theories of history in the Renaissance such as the Tudor myth as explained by Tillyard and others. There was not, however, as H. A. Kelly has pointed out, a monolithic view of history among Renaissance humanist historians such as Polydore Vergil, Hall and Holinshed. In addition to the Tudor myth, there were Lancastrian and Yorkist accounts available (Kelly, 1970). Each myth interprets this period of history in different ways indicating God's favour to the various contending dynastic forces. It makes little sense to argue that Shakespeare is a semi-official apologist for Elizabethan orthodoxies when we cannot firmly establish which ones he supported or even the precise nature of those orthodoxies. All views of the plays as orthodox Tudor propaganda strike one as odd in face of a writer who produced, in the nine plays of which *Henry V* is the culmination, a vast array of passages which exhibit cant and hypocrisy as almost inescapable attributes of a politician.

Among Shakespeare's contemporaries there was a very vigorous debate about how war could be justified and how battles were fought. A simple endorsement of chauvinism seems inherently unlikely given what we know of Shakespeare's work, for he never uncritically endorses military glory. In this very cycle of plays he has only recently considered such a search for glory, through the eyes of Falstaff, to be sheer folly, and shown us how Hotspur, who seeks to pluck bright honour from the pale-faced moon, ends up as food for worms. It also seems unlikely, given Henry's fame among Elizabethans, that Shakespeare would have undertaken the kind of satirical hatchet-job on Henry's reputation akin to his ferocious account of the fatuity of war and the baseness of Achilles in *Troilus and Cressida*.

Another strategy in salvaging the heroic reputation is to refuse to see any continuity between Prince Hal and King Henry, to sever this final play from the cycle and regard it as a fresh start. The attractive qualities of the warrior-king are celebrated and the existence of shadows stemming from our previous experience of him as manipulative prince are denied:

> Shakespeare is not asking his audience to suppose that the Hal of Eastcheap has been transformed into this paragon of learning and discretion. In this opening scene of *Henry V* he gives notice that the king is to be clearly dissociated from the Prince of *Henry IV* ... and adopts the popular explanation of a completely unpremeditated change of character at the young king's coronation. (Winny, 1968, p. 175)

> Critical confusion arises when this Henry is expected to be identical to the Henry who rejects Falstaff in *Henry IV*. Rather the king is a character very much like Hotspur as the play begins. The main difference, however, is that Henry can learn moderation. (Babula, 1977, p. 47)

> It would have been too risky to allow [Henry] to remain the ironist after he had come to the throne. Shakespeare came to terms with this situation by jettisoning the character he had created and substituting one which, though lacking all consistency, satisfied the requirements both of the chroniclers and of popular tradition. No wonder if the play constructed round him shows a great falling off in quality. (Tillyard, 1962, p. 306)

Such views make little sense, especially in this cycle of plays, where the child is father of the man by a very determined act of will.

Shakespeare started his career carrying over characters from play to play. In every case there is a continuity of character, often a fuller unfolding of the traits he had already established. It is useful for any actor playing such a character, when a cycle of plays is being presented in one season, to use all of the plays to grasp its range and development. This is true of Henry VI, Queen Margaret, Edward IV, Humphrey of Gloucester, the Bishop of Winchester, Somerset, Suffolk, Warwick, Richard of Gloucester and Elizabeth Grey in the first tetralogy. In the second one it is true also of Bolingbroke, Hotspur, Northumberland, Prince John, Falstaff, Bardolph, Pistol, Poins, Lady Percy and Nell Quickly. It is odd to deny continuity to Hal/Henry, prominent in three of the four plays, simply because he seems to undergo a most radical change of character, especially when he promises such a change and accomplishes it twice with such perfect timing. His self-control in the creation of his projected image is highlighted by contrast to the spontaneity and absence of self-control in those he exploits such as Hotspur, Falstaff and the Dauphin, who are but 'factors' to be called to a 'strict account' in each of the plays in which he appears. It is in this way that Shakespeare resolved a basic problem in the character of Henry that his sources presented to him. There was a strong tradition indicating the wild, un-disciplined youth of Henry which does not accord with the industry and extensive battle-service the chronicles record him as performing from his youth until his death. The model for the radical transformation in Henry when he assumed the crown is set out in *The Famous Victories* where the transition from madcap to sober and responsible king takes place in a matter of a few lines and in a manner that is unexplained and incredible. Shakespeare had to resolve the contradiction between two quite different people he inherited from tradition – the before and after coronation Henry – by restructuring them into one complex but coherent role. Any argument which asserts that Hal's soliloquy (*1 Henry IV*, I.ii.188–210) is simply a convention, supplied for the sake of the audience and without any connection to the psychological nature of the character, fails to register how brilliantly it resolves Shakespeare's problem. This reconciliation of the two contradictory characters is done in a manner that is the most practised element of Shakespeare's repertoire, the role-player deeply premeditating his actions in order to gain the advantage of surprise by exploiting a disguise with precise timing. Many of his major characters operate in this fashion: Hamlet, Claudius, Macbeth, Lady Macbeth, Iago, Edmund, Iachimo, Cleopatra. In the first decade of his writing also there are effective performers: Richard III, Proteus, Aaron, Petruchio, Portia, Rosalind, Mark Antony, Viola. Hal/Henry is, however, his most sustained study of the skilled role-player.

It seems likely that Shakespeare sketched out a rough plan of the tetralogy quite early. He appears to intend a play about Hal already in 1595 by his inclusion of Hotspur in *Richard II*, a character totally unnecessary to the play, who is made practically a generation younger than his model and seen from the outset as a foil to the prince. The meaning of each play subsequent to *Richard II* is enriched by the emergence of old problems in a new guise as each king must strive to play the role in a way that ensures unity rather than dissension. The cycle ends with a man far different from Richard II, who has become an extremely skilled politician in learning how to project an effective image. As we observe the construction of his performance admiration and dislike are mingled in our response. As Greenblatt phrases it:

> We are continually reminded that Hal is a 'juggler', a conniving hypocrite and that the power he both serves and comes to embody is glorified usurpation and theft; yet at the same time, we are drawn to the celebration of both the prince and his power. (Greenblatt, 1985, p. 30)

Shakespeare allows himself plenty of space to develop our oscillating responses. Henry in his three plays is, after all, the largest role Shakespeare ever wrote, provided with both the most lines and the most onstage time. He has 1,853 lines, compared to Richard Gloucester with his 1,473 lines in two plays, Hamlet with 1,422 in one play, Antony with 1,083 lines in two plays and Falstaff, who has 1,602 lines in the two plays he shares with Hal and *Merry Wives*. Hal first tries out his transformation in practice in the robbery at Gadshill and his ensuing roasting of Falstaff, capping it in an improvised play in which he pretends to be his father but is in fact rehearsing his own future transformation when he becomes king (*1 Henry IV*, II.iv). In each circumstance he juxtaposes the behaviour expected of him with a totally contrasting role to stunning effect. In the entire sequence Hal achieves surprise by his protean changes in role nearly a dozen times (Brennan, 1989, pp. 47–56). He soon transfers these skills to the court, where he promises his father 'I shall hereafter, my thrice-gracious lord,/Be more myself' (*1 Henry IV*, III.ii.92–3). He then refines his technique during the negotiations with the rebels and caps his performance as emergent hero at the Battle of Shrewsbury. In *2 Henry IV* he repeats the process all over again and when his father worries about his truancy (IV.iv.54–66), Hal, with his alchemical facility, turns to gold once more. Shakespeare devotes two scenes (v.ii and v.v) and 255 lines to Henry's public demonstration of the transformed character he had promised several thousand lines before. This process of surprise transformation is not a strategy so brilliantly devious that it is undetectable. His father, an expert in tormenting himself with burdensome anxieties, is convinced that his son, like Richard, has 'Enfeoffed himself to popularity'. Warwick, however, has more perception and is confident that Hal 'but studies his companions' and will 'in the perfectness of time,/Cast off his followers' (*2 Henry IV*, IV.iv.68–78). Comparatively few men, however, have this discernment so that this trick of transformation still works effectively on many figures in *Henry V*.

Henry is not anything so simple as a man born to be king, as Richard II took himself to be. He spent the first twelve years of his life with no expectation that he would ever be king. For some of his early years he was not with his father but was nurtured in the court of Richard II. Shakespeare presents him as a man who learns from the experiences of two other kings the dangers, delusions and anxieties inherent in the role. He never allows himself to be seduced into believing that it is a role that can be taken for granted or practised with any negligence. He approaches the role warily, concerned always to project it effectively and with different emphases on to his various audiences of aristocrats, soldiers, commoners and enemies. He realises from the outset a fundamental truth about shaping a profile of political behaviour, that if you feed an audience low expectations about your performance you can always achieve surprise by exceeding them. Out of the contradictory, haphazard traits Shakespeare found in his sources he was able to shape a complex, evolving character who adapts himself effectively to the circumstances of his time.

It can be argued that anyone who sees a performance of *Henry V* for the first time without ever having read or seen the *Henry IV* plays could make good sense of it apart from some puzzlement about the references to Falstaff in ii.i and ii.iii. For well over two hundred years the play was not presented in the context of its tetralogy. Critics eager to preserve Henry's unblemished reputation, presented for so long on stage, not surprisingly detach this play from its two forerunners and insist that Shakespeare makes a completely fresh start on the character. The Elizabethan audience, however, must have seen these plays and experienced them as a connected sequence. We can assume from the popularity of Falstaff that the plays may have been frequently revived. He had lodged a sufficient place in the audience's imagination that Shakespeare could tantalisingly promise a continuation of the Falstaff story in the French campaign – a promise he did not fulfil. The illness and death of Falstaff as reported in ii.i and ii.iii, and Fluellen's mention of his rejection in iv.vii, are placed with such devastating astuteness, and without any detailed explanation or recapitulation, that one has to accept that Shakespeare took for granted his audience's knowledge of the earlier plays in calculating his effects in *Henry V*. The flashbacks to the *Henry IV* plays used by both Olivier and Branagh in their films in order to clue in the modern audience about the relevance of the Falstaff material were obviously unnecessary to Shakespeare's audience, holding all of the sequence in mind. Every scene in the play gains depth and tension from our knowledge that the central figure is the continuous role-playing figure we have come to know in the ten acts of drama before he initiates his French campaign. It seems inconceivable that Shakespeare could show us a man who can deceive nobles, enemies, companions, his own father, Falstaff and his crew, make us relish his skill even as we experience mounting anxiety about its tendency, and then expect us to become uncritical dupes of his plain, blunt, pious warrior performance like everyone else. We are vividly reminded of the serious consequences for Falstaff, of whose continued pleasurable company we are to be denied, of submitting gullibly to Hal's role-playing. We are shown that the king's acting skill evidently continues to work on the Archbishop, the English nobles, the conspirators in the Cambridge plot, the French, the citizens of Harfleur, the French Herald, the English soldiers, the French princess, even the Chorus of the play. It works for the triumph of the English cause, but that does not mean that we should ignore the fact that it is a display of the protean skills of a fully matured politician.

It is much easier to present Henry as the unambiguous hero of long stage tradition when the play is presented separately rather than as part of the cycle. In spite of the valiant rearguard action fought for Henry as unambiguous hero, increasingly, because the play is presented in the context of part or all of the history cycle, with casting retained over several plays, the emphasis has inevitably shifted to present this play as the culminating example of the education of a skilled politician. The multifaceted nature of Henry's character has emerged with increasing effectiveness from Barry Jackson's productions in the 1920s, to the Stratford, England theatre presentation of the cycle in the early 1950s, mid 1960s, mid 1970s, to the Stratford, Ontario cycles of the 1960s and late 1970s, to the Bogdanov–Pennington English Shakespeare Company's presentation of the eight-play cycle which toured so widely through the world in the late 1980s. Such productions have established beyond doubt what Shakespeare's audience probably never questioned – the connectedness of the sequence. Alan Howard, the RSC's 1975 Henry, presented the man's education as a tentative probing, complex and anxious mastery of the role and insisted:

> I do not see any discrepancy between Hal and Henry V, between Prince and King. It is an extraordinary progression straight through. At the beginning of *Henry V* he has still not established himself as a person or a king – nobody knows which way he will jump. Almost immediately he begins questioning his position in a way Richard II might have done, but from a very different point of view. (Cook, 1983, p. 67)

Though Henry is clearly the same complex figure of the *Henry IV* plays, when he assumes the crown his relationship to the audience changes. With Hal we are privileged insiders forewarned of his manipulations and his disguises in soliloquy or by his plotting with Poins. As king he is less available, moving ever more steadily into a lonely isolation. Save for one key occasion, the soliloquy in iv.i, we have no privileged access to his mind and his masks are now manipulated to take in everyone, including us. Even as we observe Henry's great skill in accomplishing his long-term plan, Shakespeare ensures that those who go along with it will, like some of his soldiers, experience discomfort in the face of some of his more dubious manipulations and ruthless strategies. Some critics assert that Shakespeare, to contain subversion, only pretends to question authority so that he can vindicate it all the more completely in the last analysis. Others assume that Shakespeare strove to assert a conservative or reactionary set of values but in spite of himself produced evidence that indicates its inadequacies. Such critics suggest that Shakespeare is a kind of helpless weathervane, but concede that in *Henry V*,

> which is often assumed to be one where Shakespeare is closest to state propaganda, the construction of ideology is complex – even as it consolidates, it betrays inherent instability. (Dollimore and Sinfield, 1985, p. 211)

Shakespeare is, however, more radical than his critics recognise. The whole tetralogy documents the loss, with Richard II, of the concept of the inviolable sacramental nature of kingship. This is compounded by Henry IV's failure in his political manoeuvring to sustain conviction in the legitimacy of his kingship. His son, by skilled manipulation, recuperates the power of the crown's authority and achieves a spectacular but merely temporary success. Authority no longer exists, Shakespeare makes it clear, in the role itself but only in the political skill of the man who fills it.

The craft with which Shakespeare endowed Henry, in his seemingly open, artless projection of himself as a warrior for the working day, was not unique to this character. We find bluntness, genuine or adopted, in a variety of characters, such as Faulconbridge, Casca, Cassius, Iago, Apemantus and Enobarbus, and so common that Cornwall can assert that Kent's genuine openness is craftily adopted (*King Lear*, ii.ii.90–9). The poet Wyatt is known to have self-consciously deployed a bluff manner, salted his conversation with homely proverbs, and operated in a way that denied its own cunning. Sir Thomas More's foreign rivals noted his diplomatic performance was 'full of craft and subtlety' concealed 'by smooth speech and calm expression in the English way' (Greenblatt, 1980, p. 143). The diamond-in-the-rough, plain soldier performance was evidently so widespread that character books warned readers to beware of being seduced by it.

The power of this play is diminished, however, when it is presented as overtly satirical, deeply ironical, anti-war propaganda. When the play repels us, then the appeal of patriotism, that primitive male bonding to which men can always revert, loses its insidious potency. As Alan Howard observed:

> People have tried to do *Henry V* as a play glorifying war and a play condemning war, but by allowing the text to be free, without preconceptions, one discovers that the play does both those things and many more. (Beauman, 1976, p. 52)

Rabkin (1971) has suggested that the play works rather like those psychological tests of perception in which we can alternatively see the figure of a rabbit or a duck without being able to maintain the image of both at the same time. When we respond to all of the play its power to claw at us cannot be denied. Its complexity forces us to recognise that Henry is more than a Machiavellian thug and less than an unambiguous, ideal king.

## · 1 ·

# 'Unwind your bloody flag':
# The campaign proposed

The chorus fires our imaginations in the Prologue with select images which serve as emblems of the broader, heroic conflict. With the effect almost of a camera panning from one nation to another the Chorus images the French the better to define the English, just as Henry has used his cloudy youth to set off his dazzling kingship. The English are active, things in motion, urgent forces breaking out against restraint, a force like fire spreading and consuming, like horses barely held in check. Words are braided together in this opening speech to indicate the catalytic effect Henry has on his nation: fire, swelling, leashed in, crouch, hold, cram, affright, girdle, confined, upreared, parts asunder, printing their proud hoofs in the receiving earth, jumping. Critics have asserted that this invocation, so self-deprecatingly full of apology, is needed by Shakespeare to alert his audience that he is striving, in the epic range of material, to do something new in the theatre, but is aware that his stage cannot supply the requisite panoply. The Arden editor clearly regards the Chorus as the voice of Shakespeare striving to create a novel effect: 'No wonder Shakespeare . . . becomes apologetic' (Walter, 1954, p. xv). The Chorus is 'the authentic voice of the poet himself' according to Stoll (Berman, 1968, p. 103). In his revolutionary approach to drama in this play

the apologetic tone 'is quite deliberate. Shakespeare knew he was
risking the scorn of the learned and judicious spectator' (Moseley,
1988, p. 97). Such views, however, raise more problems than they
solve. Why would someone believing in the inadequacy of his
theatre, anxious about the response of his audience, seek to
advertise his problems and prompt his audience to look out for
them? In any case why would Shakespeare, already author of eight
history plays and confident dramatiser of many battles, suddenly
doubt the adequacy of his stage for the task. He does not ask his
audience to use their imagination for his tawdry staging of battles
at Orléans, Rouen, Bordeaux, Angiers, St Albans, Wakefield,
Towton, Barnet, Tewkesbury, Bosworth, Shrewsbury, nor for any
of the constant crossings back and forth across the English channel.
But above all why would he apologise and then use so few of the
resources of his well-honed and complex technique of staging
battles, which I have analysed elsewhere (Brennan, 1989, pp. 131–
208), in this the most glorious of England's victories? The prodding
of the audience's imagination, the sleight of hand of drawing it into
battle by a judicious mixture of onstage fighting with accounts of
offstage combat, is a skill Shakespeare had developed very much
further than any of his contemporaries. If Shakespeare agreed with
his Chorus about the unblemished glory of heroic action at Agincourt, if he truly felt that any staging of it would only seem a tawdry
reduction, then he would obviously have omitted any element of
the kind of ignoble action which cross-hatches the events at
Shrewsbury. But, in fact, Shakespeare quite deliberately *omits*,
either as onstage action or as reports of offstage events, many details
of the battle strategy and heroic action available in the sources
which would have reflected glory on Henry, and he *includes*
elements that produce ambiguity around Henry's action, and
presents, as the central onstage event at Agincourt, a long sequence
which is as sharp a burlesque of heroism as Falstaff's prudent
evasiveness at Shrewsbury. We cannot conceivably take these
apologies in the Prologue, which are reiterated throughout, to be
Shakespeare's, not only because of the relative absence of glorious
actions which the Chorus claims are unstageable, but because the
play has many scenes which challenge its assertion that the French
campaign involved a unified nation in unalloyed heroism.

In the language of the Prologue there are at times 'princes to act' a 'swelling scene', 'the warlike Harry' and 'two mighty monarchies' involved in stirring events. Also on this 'scaffold' there are figures so 'unworthy' that the Chorus never deigns to acknowledge their existence. Shakespeare ensures that these 'flat, unraised spirits' and 'crooked figures' are more than mere 'ciphers to this great accompt'. The Chorus laments the absence of flotillas, horses, battlements and cannons. The Victorian age with its vast crowd scenes, sumptuous costumes, crumbling walls of Harfleur and, in Calvert's 1872 production, even the horse, Crispin, undermined Chorus in a way quite different from Shakespeare's aim. Elizabethans accepted equably that this bare stage could represent places all over the known world and across a vast historical range. The Chorus also apologises for the absence of impressive costumes which, from contemporary accounts, we know Shakespeare's company was quite capable of providing. In its apologies for the 'vile and ragged foils' and 'brawl ridiculous' it seems that, instead of the chaos of war, the Chorus might prefer a pageant as crisp, dazzling and unreal as the half-time show in American football. Shakespeare recognises and shows us how a lack of glamour, which Henry exploits, can also be incorporated into the legend. The emphasis on the drab, tatty, unimpressive slovenry of the English makes the battle victory seem miraculous. Shakespeare knows, as the Chorus does not, that the supposed limitations of his stage will help him both to re-create the legend and to question it.

There has been resistance to such questioning. Richard Levin has objected to the burgeoning growth of ironic readings of Shakespeare's plays which seem to presuppose an elitist Shakespeare writing for a small minority and making fools of everyone else. He argues that we must trust Shakespeare's play and the response it has elicited in viewers and readers for 'whenever a traditional interpretation has grown up around the play over the generations, it is very likely to be close to his real intentions' (Levin, 1977, p. 157). Such a view is, as I have tried to show, inadequate in dealing with the complex history of responses to this play. In the theatre the 'traditional interpretation' was created, until recently, by presenting less than two-thirds of the text on stage, a tradition, therefore, not based on Shakespeare's play but on censored versions which exploited it for ideological purposes. In the recent history of the play Levin would, in fact, be hoist by his own petard because, increasingly, the dominant reading, creating a new tradition, is an ironical one.

The way the Chorus is 'placed' in the play is a critical factor in shaping its interpretation. The 'traditional interpretation' Levin upholds has, it is true, often been debunked excessively by ironical readings of the Chorus, as at Stratford, Connecticut in 1969. The actors came on to a playground set in casual modern clothes throwing frisbees and dribbling basketballs. The members of this street-gang eventually lay on their backs, kicked their feet in the air and hissed while the Prologue was delivered by several individuals, the group periodically intoning 'O for a muse of fire' as a refrain. The Stratford, Ontario Chorus of 1966 was performed as the equivalent of the voice in a government propaganda news-reel. It urged the audience to close ranks as the moment of decision approached and ticked off our side's virtues against the oppo-nents' bad points. In the 1984 RSC production Ian McDiarmid delivered the Prologue in a flippant tone, seeming cynically to doubt the heroism his speeches evoked. He attempted to 'natural-ise' the speeches with winks and leers and mickey-taking of the text. In the most recent Stratford, Ontario production (1989) the actors in rehearsal clothes on a bare stage stiffened to attention as, with house lights up, the orchestra struck up 'God save the King'. The poppy in the lapel of Chorus indicated he was a First World War veteran recalling its glory but also inevitably reminding the audience of the futile waste of youth in that war. At the end of the Prologue 'Jerusalem' was played and sung by the cast in unison, and the property dock at the rear was closed to make a war memorial to Harfleur and Agincourt with the printed names of the dead on it. A mother sorrowfully picked out the name of her son etched on it and was comforted by Chorus. The lifework of Shakespeare is, in considerable part, a constant struggle against what he was well aware were the appealing seductions of re-ceived views and prejudices, the vapid simplifications, the orotund rhetoric that can make men misty-eyed and gullible about the nobility of a cause. The legend about Henry, he knew, must contain some of the truth but not all of it. He has the Chorus play ostrich to alert us not to do the same. When men submit to partial truths, accepting stereotypes and failing to probe behind the beguiling surface of legend, they sacrifice part of their humanity. Productions with an overkill of irony are as much of a distortion as the tradition which ensured that the play's action reflected without question the attitudes of Chorus.

The private conversation of the prelates (1.i), a scene omitted from the quarto, is developed in three parts: (a) 1–21; (b) 22–69a; (c) 69b–98. The opening discussion of the threat to the wealth of the Church gives place to the welcoming of Henry, as a strayed sheep back to the fold, in his dramatic transformation from 'wildness' and 'courses vain' to 'sudden scholar' blessed with all the king-becoming graces. The prelates' eulogy is scarcely disinterested, for as 'a lover of the holy church' they are hopeful that he will protect them in the legislation which threatens their authority and financial interests. Because of the structure of the scene the Church's strategic offer of financial aid to promote a prospective French campaign sounds very much like a bribe to secure itself from danger. Henry's carefully placed reformation is still evidently paying dividends as we recall it did, at the end of the previous play in the tetralogy, in the cold sacrifice of Falstaff.

The threat to the Church's interests, as Holinshed recounts, was originally proposed in Henry IV's reign. Shakespeare did not invent this sly calculation of the clerics but, by adjusting the timing, he sharpened the implication in Holinshed that this threat of seizure of the Church's temporal lands was

> much noted and more feared among the religious sort, whom suerlie it touched very neere, and therefore to find remedie against it, they determined to assaie all wayes to put by and overthrow this bill: wherein they thought best to trie if they might moove the kings mood with some sharpe invention that he should not regard the importunate petitions of the commons. (Bullough, 1962, pp. 377–8)

This kind of strategy cannot simply be put down to Protestant disdain of the craft of Catholic prelates, of which there is some evidence in Shakespeare's sources. In Elizabethan times the

Church often resented the fact that it was expected to help finance
foreign wars, but in 1586, 1588 and 1593 the Archbishop of
Canterbury did contribute to military expeditions and, in encouraging generous contributions to resist the Armada, Whitgift
did so on grounds, very much like those in the days of Henry V,
that it would defuse criticism of the Church's wealth (Strype,
1822, pp. 524–6). Even though the majority would accept such
chauvinism in the Church there were probably some who were
troubled by it. Gould has urged acceptance of the clear significance of this opening: '. . . unless its intention is the obvious
cynical one, there is no intention at all' (Quinn, 1969, p. 87).
Shakespeare chooses to splice together two quite separate incidents and to reverse their historical order. The presentation of
the Dauphin's insult of a tun of tennis balls occurred at Kenil-
worth during Lent of 1414. The threats to confiscate the Church's
property took place at Leicester after 30 April 1414. In this way
he makes it clear that the Archbishop's argument in the play's
second scene about Henry's claim to the French crown, and his
offer of Church money to finance it, is shaped by the ulterior
motive, short-term pain for long-term gain, of protecting Church
property. It is hardly flattering to the Church to hear how
strongly it resists the Commons' intention of stripping its money
to provide, in part,

> relief of lazars and weak age
> Of indigent faint souls, past corporal toil,
> A hundred alms-houses right well supplied.
> (1.i.15–17)

Resisting this kind of charity is, in modern parlance, the kind of
'damage control' that can give you a black eye. We are certainly
not being led to believe that Henry is being deceived by the
archbishop into a war he does not want. Negotiations for claiming
the French crown have been opened, Canterbury has offered
money, and was broaching the legal bases on which Henry could
make his claim to the French crown when he was interrupted by
the arrival of the French ambassadors. Canterbury's tribute to
Henry's mastery of practical politics contains acknowledgement
that he has the rhetorical skills to use theory and ideology to

enhance his power (1.i.47–52). Ely seems to suggest that Henry's transformation is, perhaps, a deliberate calculation in that 'the prince obscured his contemplation/Under the veil of wildness' (1.i.63–4). The king's reformation encourages the prelates to believe that he will protect their interests, but they are not yet assured of his support. In 'the mitigation of this bill/Urged by the commons' (1.i.70–1) to strip the Church of property the king 'seems indifferent', though 'swaying more on our part'. Henry, it seems, allows the threat of legislation to hang over the Church without giving a clear signal that he will protect its interests. This prompts Canterbury to try to confirm the king's resistance to the bill, 'For I have made an offer to his majesty' (1.i.75), and that *for*, which indicates a link in a chain of cause and effect, certainly implies that the monetary support for the war is an attempt to ensure a favourable outcome for the Church's private cause. Canterbury has not yet pressed the pursuit of war because negotiations, demands and counter-offers, 'causes now in hand', are still proceeding. He assumes, however, that war is probable because he is confident that the French will reject the demands Henry has already made (1.i.95–7). The demands may have been made in a manner which ensures their rejection. Canterbury's strategy of material and ideological support for the war, in exchange for relief from the pressure of the bill in the Commons, is based entirely on his calculation that there can be no peaceful settlement with France.

It is worth noting how any problem the scene contains has, until recently, been resolved. Before this century the first scene was frequently cut. Of the last thirteen productions at the various Stratfords it was totally cut four times, cut by about a half four times, by at least a third four times. Only once was it lightly cut (SE, 1937: 9.7 per cent). The effect, in all but the last four productions (SE, 1975, 1984; SO, 1980, 1989), is to make the later offer by Canterbury of financial support for the king (1.ii.132–5) seem spontaneous rather than a public affirmation of a negotiation already broached in private to the king. In recent productions the scene has been heavily satirical, beating the audience over the head, to indicate how authorities exploit patriotism to protect their own vested interests. The prelates have been presented as sly,

clerical foxes, Canterbury lit up with glee in his political gossip
(SE, 1984), or cuddled together on a love-seat with sugar-dipped
strawberries as they planned the next war (SO, 1966), or sat in
winged armchairs over a decanter of claret (SO, 1989), or with
Canterbury dressed like a clown in a huge hooped red robe with
large yellow buttons so that he looked, to the *Time* reviewer, like
a 'cartoon of gluttony, indicating that the Church would feed on
men's lives to fatten its authority' (SC, 1969). In the BBC TV
version the clerics conferred secretly, anxiously glancing over their
shoulders, while kneeling at prayer in what was clearly hypocritical
piety. Branagh's film took the same path with Canterbury closing
a heavy door to ensure secrecy and checking on it to ensure he was
not being overheard. This is very different from the clerics as
doddering buffoons which was common in the rare pre-1960s
productions that presented the scene at all. No Elizabethan
doubted that churchmen were skilled political figures, nor should
we automatically assume that they would have received oppro-
brium for looking after their own interests. In face of a threat to
their property they have decided on a course which serves their
own ends but which, they may also be convinced, serves those of
their country. Had Shakespeare wished us to accept a totally
sanitised account he would never have included the scene in the first
place. Had he wanted to press on us an entirely satirical account,
to which recent productions have so often inclined, he would have
made his intentions even clearer. As it stands we are caught, in
the manner in which we will spend much of the play, in some
ambiguity. Holinshed gives a hint of the Church's ulterior motive
in his account of the parliament at Leicester:

> . . . the bill for dissolving of religious houses was cleerlie set
> aside, and nothing thought on but onelie the recovering of
> France, according as the archbishop had moved. (Bullough,
> 1962, p. 380)

Shakespeare's prelates are pursuing a far-reaching strategy, but it
is possible that they are being manipulated in an even further
reaching strategy of the king's. The role of reluctant figure needing
persuasion to take on weighty responsibility has been the keynote
of his career.

We are never likely to forget Henry IV's injunction to his son 'to busy giddy minds/With foreign quarrels' (2 *Henry IV*, IV.v.214–15) in order to unite his country and escape the plague of civil war. Clearly aware that warmongering will not win him the stamp of approval as an ideal prince Henry is careful to distance himself from any perception that he is the initiator of a campaign against France. Henry is also careful to ensure that the rebuff from the French is not the only motivation for war. Shakespeare has Henry order events to give himself maximum protection. When Westmoreland asks him if the French ambassadors should be admitted (I.ii.3), Henry pointedly indicates that other matters must be resolved first. By this point we know that Henry has already been offered a large sum of money by the Church to pursue war, has got Canterbury to initiate the proposal, 'Which I have open'd to his Grace at large,/As touching France' (I.i.78–9), and has allowed the archbishop to begin on and promise detailed documentation of 'The severals and unhidden passages/Of his true titles' (I.i.86–7) to the French crown. Henry wants the legality of his claim to be the basis of war rather than the French refusal of his terms. He may have heard enough of Canterbury's arguments to know they are persuasive, but they have been delivered to him in private where they cannot fully serve the need Henry has of them. His warning to the archbishop to be careful not to bend the truth or exaggerate the claims (I.ii.13–17) may stem from his awareness that others might believe that Canterbury's zeal in promoting war is driven by his desire to protect the Church's interests. His warning of the dangers inherent in waking 'the sleeping sword of war' which brings horror in its trail instantly and publicly establishes his concern for his subjects' welfare by his reluctant stance.

In the sixteenth-century books which consider justifications for war it is invariably asserted that it must always be directed at the execution of justice, and never for private revenge, and only after every course to avoid it has been tried. Because a monarch puts far more bodies at risk than his own he has to satisfy more than his private conscience in trying to determine what is a just war. Augustine was very insistent on this and Erasmus, the most famous Renaissance authority on the matter, was equally clear that invasion without provocation in pursuit of a lust for territory was indistinguishable from brigandage. The crusade to the Holy Land, which Henry IV planned and urged on his son, and which Henry V promises to his own son, is the kind of justifiable campaign which Augustine supported, but the campaign in France is a far more ambiguous matter. Many have seen Henry's behaviour in this scene as typical of the ideal prince we see in Sidney or Castiglione, a king 'who is far from trigger-happy, but cares deeply about justice . . . aware that the rightness of his cause is not one he alone can decide' (Moseley, 1988, p. 150). Other critics believe that his decision to go to war has been made before he ever enters this scene and that what we see here is his skill in public theatre. We are not given any clear signal that this is a carefully constructed performance, though everything we know about Henry makes it inherently probable. His behaviour here is reminiscent of Gloucester in III.vii of *Richard III*, a figure 'persuaded' to take action that he has meant to take from the start. One critic asserts that Machiavelli, who is quite explicit about the ruler using God and the Church to strengthen his position, would have been far readier to accept Henry as his ideological offspring than Richard of Gloucester (Manheim, 1973, pp. 168–9). Henry is far less detectable and unsettling because he has none of Richard's vice-like propensity of cynically unveiling his plans to the audience. Nowadays, no matter how strong our suspicions, we are liable to find his image-building 'no more hypocritical and ruthless than that of twentieth century politicians, even if it is no more endearing' (Wentersdorf, 1976, p. 265). Another critic has noted how characteristic his behaviour is in this scene, for he

> always proves extremely ingenious in putting the blame for his actions on somebody else: on Falstaff, on the Archbishop, on the Dauphin, on the besieged citizens of Harfleur, on whoever comes in handy not excluding God himself. (Stribny, 1964, p. 94)

However, to insist that Henry's shifting of responsibility on to others shows a lack of moral fibre is to overstate the case. It is, rather, an example of his political acumen. As the scene develops he seems to be the only figure to grasp the moral issue of the war and to be troubled by the carnage it will entail. If war is to be ventured it must be publicly seen to be just so that it can be pursued with a clear conscience. Henry takes on himself the posture of a dutiful son of the Church. In his first long speech (I.ii.8–32) he makes three references to God and uses other words which emphasise piety: 'religiously unfold', 'understanding Soul', 'conscience', 'pure as sin with baptism'. The argument here about a just war is related to Henry's debate with his soldiers in IV.i, where the king will argue that every man's conscience is his own and each man must be responsible for his own actions in war. In his warning to Canterbury, 'take heed how you impawn our person', he seems to present the opposite case, the one with which Williams will confront him, that those who promote war must be held responsible, a contradiction not surprising in such a pragmatic figure as Henry. He knows before this council opens that the archbishop will argue zealously for war, which affords him the opportunity to appear, by contrast, more wisely cautious.

The archbishop's prolix interpretation of the Salic law has divided critics of the play. Bullough (1962, p. 356) argues that Shakespeare makes no attempt to present the churchmen in an unfavourable light and that the Salic law must have had great interest for an audience which held allegiance to a female monarch. Reese (1961, p. 324) asserts that the Salic law is a dishonest contrivance of French jurists to deny the claims of Edward III and that, though the present century has made us very suspicious of excuses invented to countenance aggression, in feudal law, Henry's war was justified. Henry is certainly striving to work by the precedents of justice. It is worth remembering that on his accession he took the Lord Chief Justice as his surrogate father. In applying to the archbishop here as his adviser he seems to be doing the same, trying perhaps to avoid the lawlessness Richard II had unloosed when he seized Bolingbroke's inheritance. Other critics, however, have fastened on a flaw in the archbishop's logic. There are references in the archbishop's argument which remind us of Henry's dubious legal claim to the English crown and which are likely to have had a special significance for Shakespeare's audience and for Henry himself which the churchman did not intend. Henry is hardly likely to forget that he is the son of a usurper who

deposed a rightful king, a usurper troubled throughout his reign
by his conscience. So these references are hardly tactful: 'King
Pepin which deposed Childeric' (65), 'Hugh Capet also, who
usurp'd the crown' (69), 'Also King Lewis the Tenth/Who was
sole heir to the usurper Capet,/Could not keep quiet in his
conscience,/Wearing the crown of France' (77–80). As Hamlet
might say, 'That's wormwood'. Douglas Rain, as Henry in Langham's production (SO, 1966), started at some of these references,
making the audience aware of their relevance to his own situation.
More important than these accidental barbs, however, is the fact
that certainly some of the Elizabethan audience, who had been
given extended training by Shakespeare himself in the dynastic
problems of the English, may have noticed a deep irony in the
argument which escapes the archbishop. He says that the French
want to bar Henry's title to their throne because he inherited it
through the female line whereas their title to it is crooked and was
usurped from Henry and his progenitors because it was inherited
in precisely the same way. By this logic neither France nor
England would belong to Henry, but both would go to Mortimer.
Henry asserts a superior claim to the French throne by inheritance
through the female line. Edmund Mortimer, Earl of March, who
traced his ancestry to Philippa, daughter of Lionel, Duke of
Clarence, had, by the law of primogeniture, a better claim than the
heirs of John of Gaunt, a claim which Richard II acknowledged in
recognising him as heir presumptive. Michael Bogdanov (ESC,
1986) was so sure Shakespeare's audience would have recognised
an irony in this argument beyond the knowledge of a modern
audience that he inserted a few invented lines (after 1.i.89) to
indicate the clerics' awareness that Henry's rationale for claiming
the French crown could be used with equal effectiveness by
Mortimer to lay claim to England's crown, as well as Canterbury's
determination to deflect attention away from this weakness in the
argument.

Directors have evaded such issues, until quite recently, by often
making the speech the subject of mirth, with the courtiers yawn-
ing, shuffling, or laughing at the jumble of confusing names.
Olivier's treatment, in which Canterbury and Ely become tangled
up and lost in manuscript evidence that tumbles all over the Globe

stage, is the most widely known. In other productions the prelates have been scruffy, senile and garrulous (SE, 1951), 'doddering husks whose function is to serve as laugh fodder' (SO, 1966), a boring windbag who explains the Salic law as if it did not matter (SE, 1975). Such an approach either makes Henry's search for a legalistic base for his war farcical or it distracts an audience from those dubious elements in the argument I have outlined above. Given the extended arguments throughout Shakespeare's whole cycle of history plays as successive figures try to legitimise their claims to the crown and to dispute that of others, it seems inherently unlikely that the Elizabethan audience regarded such a huge speech as laugh-fodder. Satirising the material to another extreme (SC, 1969) also seems misguided. There the king sat on a war-machine with his knights ranged around on platforms almost drooling for combat. When the king accepted the Salic law argument the knights stretched their arms and started cawing like hawks. More recently, with a recognition of Henry's image-building political skills, it has been possible to present the Salic law argument more seriously. The prelates can be played for clarity rather than comedy (SE, 1964; SO, 1980; BBC TV, 1979; ESC, 1986). In the RSC 1984 production Henry was surrounded by 'hearties' such as Exeter baying for blood while he cautiously considered his prelates' seriously presented arguments. In the Branagh film Canterbury rattles out his discourse not with overt cynicism but with an evident awareness that his king, determined on war, needs a rapid sketch of a legal pretext. At the conclusion of the scene the prelates exchange a conspiratorial glance of satisfaction that their strategy has worked. Whatever solution to the sequence has been adopted directors have frequently made textual cuts in the Salic law argument. About half of the text was excised on some occasions (SE, 1934, 1943, 1946; SO, 1980; BBC TV; Branagh film), about a third on others (SE, 1975, 1984; SO, 1989; Olivier film), and at times it had very minor cuts (SE, 1937, 1971; SO, 1956, 1966). To play the archbishop's argument as a comic scrap-heap of dynastic rubbish 'though it make the unskilful laugh', to quote Hamlet, 'cannot but make the judicious grieve'. These figures do what people always do in wartime, they select or twist the evidence and self-righteously ignore any details that conflict with their claims. This is the game of politics to be played seriously. It is certainly not the part of those in charge to help anyone see through the game by indicating that their pretext for war is a farrago of nonsense beyond anyone's comprehension.

Canterbury's argument provides the springboard for a concerted attempt to urge a military campaign on Henry. The king allows the Chorus to swell around him without committing himself so that over a hundred lines pass (1.ii.33–135), of which he utters only one (96), a pointed insistence that he will proceed only with 'right and conscience'. His reluctance gives way only when the Church and nobility unite in urging his decision. The language embroiders a litany of repeated words in a rising anthem of battle (101–35): 'Stand for your own, unwind your bloody flag . . . mighty ancestors . . . dread lord . . . invoke his warlike spirit . . . mighty father . . . Forage in blood . . . noble English . . . awake . . . valiant dead . . . puissant arm . . . blood and courage . . . mighty enterprises . . . rouse yourself . . . lions of your blood . . . means and right . . . bodies follow . . . blood and sword and fire . . . right . . . a mighty sum'. This familiar vocabulary, we know, booms out when men start beating the drum for war. An appetite for blood mingles throughout with a view of war as a dramatic sport to be enjoyed. The Black Prince 'on the French ground play'd a tragedy' while his father on a hill 'Stood smiling' as a king of the forest might indulgently observe 'his lion's whelp/Forage in blood'. Only half his army was needed to 'entertain' the French, as the remainder had to 'stand laughing by,/All out of work and cold for action' (105–14), mere spectators of a comedy denied the more pleasurable activity of slaughter. Canterbury's view of war as a playful game is in distinct contrast to the king's description of it as 'waste in brief mortality' (28). Henry may long have had a reputation for wildness but his sobriety here is set off against the eager rashness of his prelates and nobles baying for blood. When the archbishop reiterates his offer of financial support (132–5) John Dover Wilson, in his edition of the play (1947, pp. xxi–xxii), believes that 'there is not the hint of a bribe . . . still less of his provoking the king to war in order to protect the Church's property'. Others, however, have not felt this way, especially considering that the prelate's words are a virtual repetition of the ones in 1.i when he clearly declared the offer to have precisely that purpose.

Henry's concern about leaving his kingdom vulnerable to the depredations of the Scots is contrasted with Canterbury's blithely glib dismissal of his fears (1.ii.136–73). In the sources, where Henry is more eager for war, it is Westmoreland who first raises the issue of the Scottish invasion. By allowing Henry to initiate it Shakespeare makes his king more cautious and mature than his advisers. The sequence, however, is almost invariably cut on stage. The discussion culminates in Canterbury's speech comparing 'a peopled kingdom' to a hive of honey bees (1.ii.183–212), an idea that could have been derived from a variety of sources, but is developed quite distinctively as a travesty of the views of Erasmus. Erasmus' view of the bees' commonwealth indicates that counsellors must urge a king not to fly away, not to sting, to remain in his own realm, to pursue peace rather than war, with a constant aim of clemency, a sequence of principles which the archbishop entirely reverses (Gurr, 1977, pp. 61–2). The irony inherent in this inversion of Erasmian views is often lost on stage, for the speech has been entirely excised in over half of the promptbooks I have examined.

In the ordering of events in this scene Shakespeare follows Hall rather than Holinshed. The decision to go to war if France fails to yield to his demands is made by Henry before the French ambassadors are admitted. It is clear that Henry has arranged the order of events himself to ensure that his decision seems to arrive from calm mature reasoning and with his counsellors having to share some of the responsibility for the war he intends to prosecute. Henry, of course, gets the added bonus of the Dauphin's insult. By this ordering of events it can be seen that Henry does not pursue war out of personal pique because his decision has already been made, and yet, because of the Dauphin's insult, the French appear to bring catastrophe on their own heads. This sequence is a combination of two separate incidents in the sources, the Dauphin's insult of tennis balls and the French king's reply to Henry's terms at a later date. The Dauphin's jibe at Henry's youth hardly accords with history for in 1414 Henry was, at twenty-seven, nine years older than the French prince. Henry is able

once more to capitalise on his transformation from reveller to 'a
Christian king/Unto whose grace our passion is as subject/As our
wretches fett'red in our prisons' (1.ii.241–3). With measured
control of his anger Henry makes the Dauphin seem as rashly
mistaken as Hotspur (Bogdanov in his production of the cycle
doubled the two roles, which made the connection neatly). The
ambassadors will report his transformation with the same open-
mouthed awe Vernon had once conveyed to Hotspur about this
'feathered Mercury' on a 'fiery Pegasus' able 'to witch the world'
(*1 Henry IV*, iv.i.97–110). Proving once again to be 'bright metal
on a sullen ground', Henry is determined to 'dazzle all the eyes of
France' (1.ii.279). In his witty rejoinder on the tun of treasure he
shifts responsibility away yet again from himself, for it is the
Dauphin's soul that stands 'sore charged for wasteful vengeance'
(1.ii.283) which will bring grief to widows, husbands, mothers,
sons and those 'yet ungotten and unborn'. In the gift of tennis balls
the Dauphin impugns Henry's manliness to imply a lack of sexual
potency. The habit of scorning their opponents' virility is common among both the French and the English in the crass locker-
room boasting that flourishes throughout the play. The French
ambassadors do not know that Henry has already made his
decision before he received the insult. In the audience's eyes
Henry is a chameleon who projects an image to impress the
English and the French for different reasons. To the English
nobles, once uncertain and troubled by his madcap antics, he is a
sober, attentive sifter of advice who is cautious in face of *their*
exuberance. To the French he is a man in accord with *their*
chivalric values stiffened in angry resolve by a stupid insult. As we
watch Henry carefully shaping his image we recognise that this is
how legends are made. From his first soliloquy in the cycle
(*1 Henry IV*, i.ii.188–210) Henry indicates his awareness of how
to play to an audience. In asserting his resolution to fight France
he is aware that he is playing to the biggest audience of all –
history. He will deserve a tombless death if he fails to enact a
valiant conquest that will fill many chronicles (1.ii.228–33). He is
careful, of course, not to define his success as dependent on his
personal valour, for it can only be achieved 'by God's grace' (262),
'within the will of God' (289), by giving thoughts 'to God as well

as France' (302–3), ensuring in all endeavours that they keep 'God before' (307). We have no reason to suspect the sincerity of Henry's piety, but we have no reason either to believe that it is not designed to impress his audience. His constant references to God and his fastening of responsibility for war as often as possible on others suggest not only calculation but deep anxiety. He may be resistant to taking the blame for any further potential crimes because he is in anguished uncertainty, as iv.i reveals, about whether there is punishment still to be meted out to him for his father's crime of usurpation. It is worth bearing this in mind when responding to complex scenes such as i.ii.

On the surface this scene seems to show Henry being carried along to war by an irresistible tide. Underneath we are allowed to suspect that this tide may be one Henry has helped to create by his unobtrusive arrangement of the events it contains: his allowing the Church to dangle uncertain of his protection of their interests; his awareness that the Church will offer him financial support for the war; his ensuring that the dynastic issue is fully outlined in public council; his seeming worry about a Scots' invasion, which drives his nobles and churchmen to a further urging of war; his probable anticipation of a French refusal to his demands; his delaying of the reception of that message until it can come in to reinforce the decision collectively made; his leaping on the Dauphin's insult to provide his climactic peroration promising war. Unfortunately, the full articulation of these details is rarely available on stage. All but one of the productions at the various Stratfords in the last sixty years, as well as the BBC TV production, have cut almost a third or more of the scene (SE, 1937 cut 14.5 per cent). Olivier cut 52 per cent and Branagh's film cut 65 per cent.

In Act i Shakespeare includes details that the Chorus ignores to reveal to us the complex political skills Henry needs to give the appearance of the straightforward hero of probity in which the Chorus believes. The subtlest effect of this for a leader is to conceive a policy which he believes serves the country's interest and then allow others to 'discover' it so that they become assured of its efficacy by having to convince him. Such a tactic is the mortar binding a strong consensus together, for it flatters subjects into the belief that they have a hand in guiding state affairs. It

demands of them both commitment and responsibility to ensure
that the policy succeeds. Shakespeare uses this pattern of behaviour among his master manipulators. It is how Ulysses works
on the Greeks, Cassius on Brutus, and Mark Antony on the crowd
in the forum. It is also how Vincentio induces Isabella to forgive
Angelo as he urges a revenge on her that he wishes her to resist.
Prospero increases the ardour of Ferdinand and Miranda for each
other by seeming to resist the union he intends them to make. In
*Henry V* Shakespeare induces oscillating responses in us to
indicate that we can submit to a simple view of heroism only by a
wilful act of *naïveté* which ignores much of the evidence. We are
already at the beginning of the modern world, in which every
action of a leader is shaped for public consumption and the most
successful politician is the one whose calculations are the most
difficult to detect. Shakespeare's shaping of Act 1 draws on
Holinshed's view that Henry was possessed of the following:

> Such wit, such prudence, and such policie withall, that he never
> enterprised any thing, before he had fullie debated and forecast
> all the main chances that might happen, which doone with all
> dlligence and courage he set his purpose forward. (Bullough,
> 1962, p. 407)

Henry appears in eleven of the play's scenes and in five of them
(ii.ii, iii.iii, iv.i, iv.vii and iv.viii), scenes often heavily cut in
production, he is very clearly projecting roles and doing so for
a great variety of purposes – trapping traitors, browbeating
enemies, eliciting the views of his soldiers, playing a joke on one of
them. The two major scenes in which we can suspect he is acting,
without fully being able to confirm it, are his first and last scenes
in the play, the beginning of the French campaign and the closing
of it.

The opening of Chorus II (1–11) pictures an eager nation
girding its loins for war. As in Chorus 1 there is emphasis on the
urgency of physical action: 'now' thrice repeated (1, 3, 8), 'on fire'
(1), 'thrive' (3), 'horse' (5), 'winged heels, as English Mercuries'
(7), 'expectation' (8). The king is called, with cosy familiarity,
'Harry' – a term to imply 'one of us', a friend to his people. The
French, by contrast, seem to be drained of blood and, rather than

stirring to martial challenge, stoop to bribing English traitors to conspire against Henry. The Chorus prepares us for the scene in Southampton 'now' (35) and is eager to transport us to France (37–42), confident that there is nothing of further significance to note. But Shakespeare keeps us in London with the Eastcheap laggards. It is true they are preparing for France, but to say that they are 'the youth of England' or that they are 'on fire' is to ignore the content of II.i and II.iii, for which the Chorus does not prepare us at all. Trevor Nunn believes that the exciting myths and fictions the Chorus presents are deliberately set in contrast to the more real, harder, cooler, more ambiguous events we witness in the play. Ralph Berry, interviewing him, calls the Chorus the Official Version, a public relations strategy of over-protection for Henry, played off against the play's blend of official and unofficial events (Berry, 1977, pp. 49–58). There has developed recently a habit, now rigidifying into a tradition, of breaking up some of the Choruses and distributing lines in parcels as narrative bridges between various scenes. Quite often nowadays we find part of this Chorus (1–11) placed before II.i and the rest of it before II.ii (SE, 1975, 1984; SO, 1956, 1966, 1989; ESC, 1986). The Olivier film split this Chorus, though it cut all reference to the traitors. The Branagh film carries even further the pattern developed on the stage. The same split has been used when conflations of II.i and II.iii have been introduced (SO, 1956, 1989), or the Chorus has been transposed to preface II.ii rather than II.i (SO, 1980). All of these adjustments betray the effect of Shakespeare's text where an emblematic hymn of patriotism promises heroism and the Cambridge conspiracy as preface to the channel crossing and, instead, we are first given an absurd quarrel in the Boar's Head. Only when the Chorus delivers its chauvinist account in one continuous sequence is Shakespeare's effect achieved. Instead of bathing in the promised pure stream of national glory we find ourselves in something more akin to rivulets of mud. Some of that effect is often achieved by stage business as when, after the evocation of English troops as shining crusaders, they arrive staggering drunk and pinching ladies' bottoms (SO, 1966), or when the Chorus's assertion of 'dreadful preparation' (13) gets a laugh because of the clownish antics of the Eastcheap lads (SE,

1984; ESC, 1986). There are four scenes in Act II which contribute
529 lines to the play. The Chorus prepares for a good deal of the
content of II.ii and II.iv, though the French council is not at all
shaking with fear as it asserts (12–15). The material of II.i and II.iii,
not surprisingly, is far beneath its elevated glance, yet those scenes
comprise 35.9 per cent of the act, which is a considerable chunk of
evidence to overlook. In the BBC TV production a specific point
was made of having the Chorus urge us only to attend to its sunny
account. Bardolph entered to open II.i before the Chorus had
finished so that its final two lines, preparing us for the king's
emergence at Southampton, implied that the Eastcheap rabble
would spoil the 'real' story.

In II.i we are given, at a very low level, a parodic parallel to
Henry's approach to the French campaign in I.ii. In both scenes
there is argument about the possession of a piece of property, in
one case Henry's prior claims on dynastic grounds to France, in
the other about Nell Quickly who was troth-plight to Nym but
has been married by Pistol. There is a parodic connection forward
also to II.ii since Pistol has betrayed Nym by doing a deal behind
his back just as the conspirators have betrayed Henry by doing a
secret deal with France. The king responds to the Dauphin's
calculated insult with steely calm which eventually modulates into
hammering threats (I.ii.259–97). Nym tries to suggest menace
behind his calm control but we gather that he 'dare not fight' and
that, in spite of his assertions of valour, his sword has been used
principally to 'toast cheese' (II.i.6–8). The witty threats of Henry
relating tennis to warfare are contrasted here by the more basic
insults of Pistol and Nym 'pish for thee, Iceland dog' (II.i.39–40),
'egregious dog? O viper vile!' (44), 'I would prick your guts a
little' (56). It requires only Bardolph to unsheathe his sword for
them to resort gratefully to continuing abuse rather than sword-
play. When Pistol agrees to pay a 'noble' to Nym we may recall
how the quarrel between Church and Parliament is resolved by
the payment of a 'mighty sum'. We will see the windy excesses of
competitive braggarts throughout the play in Pistol's relations
with Fluellen and Le Fer and in the argument of Macmorris with
Fluellen, as well as among the blustering French noblemen,
especially the Dauphin. These strutting figures help to define by

contrast the usually modest, impersonal demeanour of the king, who rarely makes such splenetic assertions about his honour.

The nature of ii.i and ii.iii clearly invalidates the claims of all those critics who assert this play to be a fresh start erasing our memories of Hal. The purpose and impact of these scenes disappears entirely if they are not related to the context Shakespeare very obviously takes for granted. When we enter this scene we have no means of knowing that the promise made at the end of the previous play in this cycle is not going to be kept:

> If you be not too much cloy'd with fat meat, our humble author will continue the story with Sir John in it . . . where, for anything I know, Falstaff shall die of a sweat, unless already 'a be kill'd with your hard opinions.
>
> (Epilogue, *2 Henry IV*, 25–9)

The mention of a demise for Falstaff, which is converted into a non-appearance, may indicate that Shakespeare was already considering that Pistol might be a less disruptive rogue on the campaign trail. Some critics believe that an earlier version of the play may have contained Falstaff. They claim there are lines appropriate to him in Pistol's part, but that Shakespeare had to write Falstaff out of it when Will Kempe, who probably played the role, left the company abruptly. As Gary Taylor, in his Oxford edition of the play (1982, p. 20), has pointed out, there is no evidence to support this theory and it is equally possible that Kempe left the company because Shakespeare had decided not to continue the role of Falstaff in this play. In ii.i, the boasting, insults and pretended valour of Nym, Pistol and Bardolph recall us to a familiar world. The news of Pistol's marriage to Mistress Quickly makes us anticipate the arrival of Falstaff to share in the merriment. We know that Falstaff has been humiliated by Henry, but he survived earlier roastings in the Boar's Head (*1 Henry IV*, ii.iv, *2 Henry IV*, ii.iv) so we might hope for one more resilient resurrection from the dead, as at Shrewsbury (*1 Henry IV*, v.iv). In this sequence in ii.i we might expect him to arrive to settle the quarrel of Nym and Pistol and to prepare for France. Had Shakepeare not wanted us to canvass such expectations he could have mentioned Falstaff's sickness at the outset of the scene. The

jolting news that we are to be denied his presence focuses our
minds on the extent of the damage to Falstaff caused by the king's
rejection. Shakespeare takes our memory of it so much for granted
that he does not even have to mention Sir John's name in the first
news of his illness. The Boy simply refers to him as 'my master'
(II.i.79) and the Hostess asserts only that 'the king has kill'd his
heart', which recalls to us that dramatic confrontation and the
king's searingly harsh speech (*2 Henry IV*, v.v.48–73) in response
to Falstaff's adoring greeting 'My king! my Jove! I speak to thee,
my heart!' It was essential to the success of Henry's 'transformation' that Falstaff be rejected as publicly as possible to lodge it in
everyone's mind. A word in private in the king's chambers would
not be enough. In the scapegoat ritual Falstaff is banished 'on pain
of death' as Henry's misleader, which the Lord Chief Justice translates into a sentence to the Fleet prison. This deepens the ambivalent
feelings we have had about Hal from the outset as a ruthless
politician. Falstaff is an anarchic figure who himself also provokes
ambiguous feelings, especially when, in exploiting the press-gang,
he coldly sacrifices simple rustics for cash. We warm to some of his
antics and to his resilience even as we recognise the political
necessity of holding him at arm's length. Henry uses him, like
Hotspur, as a 'factor' to be fattened up for slaughter, but Falstaff
also, to a large degree, misleads himself. The disturbing public
rejection is performed for the maximum benefit it brings to Henry
with little thought of the distress it might cause Sir John, though of
course Falstaff himself is as feckless in exploiting everyone around
him. Such deliberate cruelty is often a component of political necessity but it is difficult to adopt a cynicism which does not flinch at
it, especially when we hear that the rejection is virtually a death-
blow to Falstaff. Pistol prompts our anticipation of Sir John's
death: 'Let us condole, the knight, for, lambkins, we will live'
(II.i.126). The hint of selfishness is typical of the Eastcheap crowd.
Pistol sees the approaching gravy-train when, as sutler to the camp,
in his exercise of graft, 'profits will accrue' (II.i.109). They can
afford to condole the knight because they can get in on a good thing
denied to him. It is the kind of egotism in which Falstaff has himself
specialised, especially in his Gloucestershire adventures.

The precise relevance of this scene is always clear when this play

is presented as part of a continuing cycle. Few productions entirely cut this scene, even when the play is presented independent
of its cycle. I know of only two in the last sixty years which have
omitted it (Mermaid Theatre, 1960; SO, 1989), the latter conflating a few lines of ii.i with ii.iii but cutting all references to
Falstaff's sickness and death in order, presumably, to make room
for the First World War songs that were inserted, a reverse
alchemy of turning gold into dross. The scene prompts our memory of how Henry sacrificed friendship to calculation just before
we see him, with the conspirators, on the receiving end of the same
experience, an irony we appreciate when he recoils in furious
outrage at such betrayal.

Anyone who considers that Henry has left behind his habitual
cunning in role-playing and setting up undeclared plays is reminded very forcibly of the old Hal in ii.ii. In the opening
sequence (1–11), it is clear that he and his nobles are aware of the
conspiracy the Chorus speaks of. Some are surprised that Henry
does not instantly arrest the traitors. In Holinshed the exposing of
the plot is dealt with in seven words, 'wherefore he caused them to
be apprehended' (Bullough, 1962, p. 384). The opening of the
scene dispels any suspense about the identity of the conspirators
and their fate and so, it is argued, the scene dramatises 'the
ascendancy of the public welfare over that most despicable of
all private crimes against the social order, treason' (Saloman,
1980, p. 347). It has been suggested that his trapping of the traitors
is not merely a fondness for role-playing but follows a recommended procedure for dealing with treason best exemplified in
the prescription of Machiavelli in his *Art of War* (Jorgensen,
1956, p. 98). In this cat-and-mouse game, elaborated for fifty-
seven lines (ii.ii.20–76), Shakespeare underlines Henry's continuing theatrical skills in a demonstration of political shrewdness
designed to impress his noblemen. By eliciting the traitors' severe
condemnation of the man who railed at the king through an excess
of wine Henry lures them to their own destruction. This technique of letting people damn themselves out of their own mouths
is very common in Shakespeare: the lords in *Love's Labour's
Lost* entrap themselves, as do Beatrice, Benedick, Malvolio and
Bertram in other comedies; Saunder Simpcox is entrapped by

Duke Humphrey (*2 Henry VI*), Valentine by the Duke of Milan
(*The Two Gentlemen of Verona*), Shylock by Portia (*The
Merchant of Venice*), and Angelo by Vincentio (*Measure for
Measure*). Perhaps the clearest anticipation of Henry's trap here,
apart from his earlier ensnaring of Falstaff in II.iv of both parts of
*Henry IV*, is in *Richard III*. When Hastings suggests execution as
a response to Gloucester's enquiry 'what they deserve/That do
conspire my death' (*Richard III*, III.iv.61–2), he prepares the
death warrant peremptorily issued to him within a dozen lines.
When these traitors to Henry read of their discovered treachery in
their commissions they are often, on stage, instantly surrounded
by a circle of swords (SE, 1984), or find cocked revolvers at their
necks (SO, 1989). Here again we have a characteristic example of
Henry's habit of shifting responsibility on to others, a need for
self-justification, which a number of critics see as his defining
quality. It is not Henry who refuses mercy but they themselves
who have advised against it. He emphasises the monstrosity of the
crime by featuring himself as the victim of ingratitude for the great
favours extended to them.

A number of critics and several productions have presented
Henry's accusation here as deeply heartfelt and part of the growing
personal costs to Henry that public office demands. Alan Howard
(SE, 1975) indicated Henry was deeply shaken to the core, the first
of many examples of a man passionately strained by the demands
of office. Kenneth Branagh (SE, 1984) revealed an emotionally
volatile nature, and physically forced Scroop to his knees, modified
in his film to slamming Scroop down on a table and lying on top of
him to express his furious outrage. In the BBC TV production
Henry displayed a quiet, masterly control which impressed his
nobleman and reduced Scroop to tears of shame. It has also been
played with the cold contempt of a ruthless politician (SO, 1980).
However the scene is played, its complex mixture of emotion and
strategy is often sacrificed by extensive cutting. Olivier's film cut
the whole sequence and most productions have cut a quarter or
more of the scene. It is useful to remember that Henry yet again
chooses a situation which ensures the most public demonstration
of his sense of injury. In Holinshed the exposure of treachery is in
two stages; Henry exacts a confession and a motive, 'a great summe

of monie', and condemns the traitors; only then are his nobles made aware of the treachery he has uncovered in his private examination. Many critics accept Henry's purposes at face value. The French are siding with the Devil in opposing Henry and the traitors enact 'another fall of man' by joining them (Dean, 1981, p. 25). The traitors are made 'responsible for their inner values in the same way that soldiers are for their souls upon entering battle' (Toliver 1965, pp. 72–3). In emphasising the deception possible in close relationships Shakespeare approaches 'one of the tragic themes' (Tillyard, 1962, p. 313). Another critic believes it is an opportunity for Shakespeare to signal the deep insecurity driving all his actions before Agincourt which makes him 'fight for his title before he fights or works for the commonwealth' (Gurr, 1977, p. 67). The huge display of anger against Scroop as an actor skilled in deception comes oddly from a figure who is himself an expert in this mode. This speech (ii.ii.79–150), the longest in the play, is frequently heavily edited in production, often losing up to half of its lines, which unfortunately distorts the proportions of the speech. Henry's indictment of Grey and Cambridge takes eight lines (85–93), but there are fifty lines aimed at Scroop, the man who bore 'the key of all my counsels' and knew 'the very bottom of my soul', which is Shakespeare's elaboration of a couple of sentences about this special friendship in Holinshed (Bullough, 1962, p. 384). The lengthy vilification of Scroop is entirely Shakespeare's invention which allows Henry to focus on the treachery of his bosom friend, thus diverting attention away from the unstated political motives of the conspiracy.

There was a much more significant basis for this conspiracy, of which the historical Henry and Shakespeare were certainly aware. Holinshed acknowledges, as does *The Mirrour for Magistrates*, that Cambridge was not merely bought by French gold but undertook the plot in the hope of bringing

> to the crowne his brother-in-law Edmund, earle of March, as heire to Lionell duke of Clarence: after the death of which earle of March, for diverse secret impediments, not able to have issue, the earle of Cambridge was sure that the crowne should come to him by his wife, and to his children of hir begotten. (Bullough, 1962, p. 386)

Shakespeare does allow Cambridge to assert that gold of France
was not his motive and to hint vaguely at another intention
(II.ii.155–7). The basic facts relating Mortimer and Cambridge are
introduced on several occasions and with recurrent emphasis in
the cycle of Shakespeare's plays so that many must have noted the
omission or suppression of the information here as having a
special significance. It has been pointed out that *Sir John
Oldcastle*, performed by the Admiral's men late in 1599, a few
months after *Henry V* was first acted, was very clear about the
dynastic aspect of this plot and presented Cambridge arguing that
his wife has a better claim to the crown than Henry (Wentersdorf,
1976, pp. 278–9). By concealing this dynastic aspect Shakespeare
may be signalling, to an audience perfectly familiar with it, a conspiracy of silence shared by Henry and the traitors for different
reasons. All three of the conspirators were connected to enemies of
Henry IV and hoped to assassinate his successor and replace him
with the Earl of March. Cambridge had been married to March's
sister, Grey and Scroop had connections to the Percies and to Glen-
dower. Richard Scroop, archbishop of York beheaded by Henry
IV in 1405, was uncle to the Scroop Henry V had taken as his bosom
friend. Henry's fury at Scroop's betrayal may be both heartfelt and
a useful smokescreen diversion from the political implications of
the conspiracy. Holinshed gives Shakespeare warrant for this
interpretation in noting that the traitors were willing to 'confess'
they had conspired for money the better to protect Mortimer and
to give the king no reason to pursue the lives of their families whose
titles and properties would then be forfeited leaving the widows
and children destitute. To publicise the fact that Cambridge's son
had a better claim to the crown than Henry would have jeopardised
the boy's life. Holinshed clearly states that many divined the
dynastic motive despite the pretence of the seduction of French
gold, and this smokescreen worked for Cambridge when

> he feigned that tale, desiring rather to save his succession than
> himselfe, which he did in deed: for his sonne Richard duke of
> Yorke not privelie but openly claimed the crowne, and Edward
> his sonne both claimed it and gained it. (Bullough, 1962, pp.
> 384–5)

Cambridge had been in his grave forty-six years when, in 1461, Edward IV had parliament reverse the judgement on the dead traitor. Shakespeare had dramatised these aspects of the Plantagenet triumph at the beginning of his career in *2 Henry VI*, II.ii, and *3 Henry VI*, I.i, II.ii, II.vi. Henry V can know nothing of this, of course, but he is certainly wise in concealing the real motive of a conspiracy which on the eve of his campaign uses the same grounds on which he is claiming the French crown, succession derived through the female line, to assert that the Earl of March has a better claim to the English crown than he does.

It has been claimed by Dollimore and Sinfield (1985, p. 216) that this play is only in one sense about national unity for its obsessive preoccupation is with insurrection from almost every quarter. Shakespeare does not present Henry as a figure who has buried all awareness that his crown is subject to dispute. In his prayer at Agincourt he acknowledges it as his deepest anxiety and greatest threat to his success in battle. In that soliloquy he does not quite hide from himself his fears about his crown behind a resentful sense of the burden of his isolation. That sense of loneliness is first broached in his tirade against Scroop, which deflects attention from the dynastic issue to focus attention on his personal losses sacrificed to his duties. Henry sees himself as a man apart, has always held himself apart for his own ultimate advantage, and is even more chary of personal relationships after Scroop's betrayal. The outrage Henry feels at Scroop suggests that he feels himself to be a victim almost of witchcraft: 'this vile man . . . savage and inhuman creature . . . practis'd on me for thy use . . . spark of evil . . . Treason and murder . . . two yoke-devils . . . cunning fiend . . . the voice in hell . . . other devils . . . botch and bungle up damnation . . . that same demon that hath gull'd thee thus . . . Another fall of man' (II.ii.94–142). Henry, like Iago, is a brilliant improviser and steers around the obvious explanation of the conspiracy so that, in seeming bafflement, he plucks an explanation of Scroop's behaviour – that the devil made him do it – out of thin air. There is something here akin to Richard II's suggestion that he is a Christ betrayed by Judas and Pilate (*Richard II*, IV.i.167–71, 237–42). Richard's accusations, however, are made as he is losing his throne, Henry's as he is securing his. To Henry,

Scroop 'seemed' dutiful, grave, learned, religious and replete with exactly those virtues Canterbury ascribed to his king in 1.i. In spite of his huge tirade Henry insists he seeks no personal revenge (174), but wants only to protect his realm from ruin. Henry again grounds his actions not in his own desires but in forces external to himself, for the revelation of the plot indicates God's concern that nothing should hinder the campaign (II.ii.185–91).

Falstaff's death, recorded in the next scene, reminds us that the experience of the traitors is, in some ways, a highly condensed version of his relationship to Henry. Sir John had promised 'I'll be a traitor then, when thou art king' (*1 Henry IV*, 1.ii.141) and, trapped by Henry, he pays for his presumption. Like the traitors, Falstaff is so absorbed in playing his own role well that he is unaware that Henry's role-playing is even better. The conspirators think to display their zeal by insisting on the punishment of the drunk who abused Henry. When Falstaff rushes to the coronation of his 'Jove' he worries that his dishevelled appearance will count against him, but then considers it shows his 'devotion' as he stands

> stained with travel and sweating with deslre to see him;
> thinking of nothing else, putting all affairs else into oblivion, as
> if there were nothing else to be done but to see him.
>
> (*2 Henry IV*, v.iv.24–7)

He is completely unprepared to be himself assigned to oblivion when he finds that there is everything else to be done but to see him. The conspirators, too, are publicly humiliated when warm friendship turns to frosty condemnation. Falstaff is not delivered to execution, of course, but we have to wonder if he deserves death as much as the traitors do. The traitors pretend to close companionship with Henry while pursuing hidden goals and personal profit. Falstaff dies as the victim of a similar kind of betrayal by Henry. A sad, elegiac quality to the scene induces us to think sombrely of the king's harsh rejection of Falstaff. A countercurrent of comic ideas, both intentional and unintentional, takes a little of the sting out of death, and arouses memories of that Eastcheap world where absurdity, earthy vitality and folly were inextricably fused. The audience shares in the mingling of laughter with tears of those on stage.

A connection with the previous scene is made by speculation about whether Falstaff is in heaven or hell, an issue on which Bardolph is uncertain but about which the Hostess displays great confidence. Henry has just indicated at length how the saintlike-seeming Scroop has had traffic with devils who won him to damnation so easily that they boasted in 'vasty Tartar' about it. Falstaff, in Henry's tirades, has constantly been associated with damnation as 'that grey iniquity, that father ruffian', 'that old white-bearded Satan' (*1 Henry IV*, II.iv.432–47). In rejecting him Henry advised Sir John 'Fall to thy prayers' for 'the grave doth gape/For thee thrice wider than for other men' (*2 Henry IV*, v.v.48–54). Everything we have known about Falstaff suggests he has damned himself to hell, and has done so with only very occasional regret. This 'stuff'd cloak-bag of guts, this swoll'n parcel of dropsies', is, however, reduced to a figure of frailty by the approach of death. The Hostess's account begins with a mala-propism that makes us smile – Arthur's bosom for Abraham's – an exquisitely apposite mistake given the distance we suspect Falstaff is from God and from the chivalric code of Camelot. But the account quells our smiles, takes hold of us and turns us like the tide to which the death is timed. As Vickers (1968, pp. 157–8) has noted of the Hostess's 'uncomprehending bawdy', her eccentricities of speech in this sad context are more touching than an unambig-uously sorrowful epitaph might be, enfolded as they are in the solemnity of the moment. The anarchic, irrepressible hedonist is finally quietened and helpless as any 'christom child'. The details of fumbling with the sheets, and the pastoral references to 'flowers' and 'green fields', combine the feebleness of age with the innocence of youth which, augmented by his smile, creates a sense of peace. This calm submission reminds us of Canterbury's description of the transformation in Henry:

> . . . his wildness, mortified in him,
> Seem'd to die too; yea, at that very moment,
> Consideration like an angel came
> And whipp'd the offending Adam out of him.
> 
> (I.i.26–9)

Falstaff, an offending Adam, seeks a forgiveness from God for his sinful past that he was unable to gain from his king. We slip from this solemnity towards laughter when the Hostess assures Sir John that, as regards God, there is 'no need to trouble himself with any such thoughts yet' (21). She is trying to assure him of recovery, but her phrasing unintentionally implies a pragmatic view that thinking of God can be postponed to the last minute when no other options are open. Feeling under the clothes up his body she registers the cold progress of death, skirting a sexual implication of 'stone', to give us a forceful image of the parting between two old friends who have had such a long association. When Nym says he has heard Sir John cried out against sack, the Hostess confirms what we might have thought impossible, especially in memory of that longest speech of his dramatic career on the properties of 'excellent sherris' (*2 Henry IV*, iv.iii.85–122). The Hostess denies the rumour that he cried out against women in an amusing linguistic salad, 'carnation' for 'incarnate', which evokes the scarlet woman, the Whore of Babylon, triggered by 'rheumatic' which sounds like Rome-atic, a malapropism, possibly, for 'lunatic'. She admits that Falstaff did in some sort 'handle' women, talk of them on his deathbed. This mashing of the language presents us with an unfamiliar repentant figure railing against sack, talking of women and Catholicism (a teasing reference to his progenitor Oldcastle and the Lollards) even as it rouses our memories of the irreligious, womanising, 'huge bombard of sack'. Falstaff has evidently finally responded to Doll Tearsheet's question 'when wilt thou leave fighting a days and foining a nights, and begin to patch up thine old body for heaven?' (*2 Henry IV*, ii.iv.221–3).

The flood of memory is momentarily fixed by that jest of his the Boy recalls about Bardolph's nose (40–2). There is also a sharper comment, which amid the sentiment may seem mean-spirited, when Bardolph asserts that his liquor-fired red nose is 'all the riches I got in his service' (44), reminding us how much Falstaff exploited others. His friends often came out on the short end but his monstrous vitality often made it seem worthwhile. In the end Falstaff was not as effective as Henry in sacrificing everything to self-interest and so his heart was broken. Pistol's command 'Let us to France, like horse-leeches, my boys,/To suck, to suck, the very blood to suck' (55–6) is one that Falstaff would have made had he survived to join the French campaign. In the ignoble aspects of the coming campaign the turkey-cock strutting betokens bone-headed stupidity rather than the inspired vitality and imagination of Falstaff, so that we feel a sense of loss at his death though we submit to the inevitability of it. We carry with us the arresting image of him as a humbled repentant man, 'the only moment in the play that touches the heart' (Ornstein, 1972, p. 201), a sobering reminder of death amid the exuberance for battle. At an earlier battle, Shrewsbury, Hal assured Sir John 'thou owest God a death' and received the reply ' 'Tis not due yet; I would be loath to pay him before his day' (*1 Henry IV*, v.i.127–8). On payment day, as Falstaff finds, and as others find later in this play, there is no ducking the gravity of the situation. As all theorists on a king's duties insisted, any leader who pursues war must bear a heavy responsibility no matter how much he strives to avoid it and fasten it on others, for its principal harvest is death.

This scene, rarely cut on stage, is so brilliant that one is inclined to believe that Shakespeare only promised to continue Falstaff's story in the Epilogue to *2 Henry IV* so as to disappoint hopes and make the shock of his death even more effective. To quell our doubts about Henry's cold indifference Shakespeare could have shown the king visiting the dying Falstaff, or, failing that, at least receiving news of his old companion's death. But Henry never registers any knowledge of it in the play. Shakespeare could, of course, have made this indifference even more explicit by having Henry receive the news and dismiss it as a matter of no consequence, but he does not do that either. Though the material about Falstaff could have been presented in one scene, and has often been rearranged so on the stage, Shakespeare could not resist the irony of setting it out in two phases around Henry's handling of the traitors to remind us of the effect and the cost of the king's skills in shaping his own image.

## · 2 ·

# 'The game's afoot':
# The campaign begins

On stage the French court in II.iv is usually dressed lavishly in velvets and brocades in gold and rich blues, embossed with *fleur-de-lis*, the more striking in contrast to the dress and style of the Eastcheap sequence just concluded. Picture-book costumes were used by Farrah (SE, 1975) to show a sophisticated, civilised people, an effect used also in the Olivier film and the BBC TV production. In the 1986 ESC production the French king's opening line, 'Thus come the English', spoken balefully, got a laugh because the Eastcheap ruffians, Pistol carrying a suitcase inscribed 'Pistol's Enterprises' and the rest wrapped in Union Jack vests and shirts, were a clear reference to the invading armies of football hooligans on the continent in recent times. Bogdanov presented the French in elegant white linen suits at their ease sipping wine in a garden setting. The French often appear on stage in bright, heraldic costumes, the better to express Shakespeare's emphasis on their archaic, chivalric values exhibited in the touchiness and vain preening of their competitive nobles. Their feudal sense of honour, based on class and heredity, contrasts with Henry's seductive suggestion (IV.iii.60–7) that nobility is attainable by anyone whose deeds deserve it. In the French army we see only aristocrats; in the English army Henry endeavours to weld nobles and yeomen into a compact unity. Charles VI is often presented as a fearful, feeble-minded figure (SE, 1946, 1951; Olivier's film), carried on a litter (SO, 1956), in a nightdress (SE, 1984), and though on occasion he is allowed to show flashes of his former power (SO, 1966, 1980, 1989; Branagh's film), there is an implication of an effete quality in the French. The Dauphin is usually played as an arrogant young fool who irritates his maturer fellow noblemen. Henry's adversaries are presented more favourably by Shakespeare than by many of his chronicle sources. There have been unsuccessful stage attempts to make them seem formidable: presenting them on stilts in something resembling blue hockey uniforms (SC, 1969), or as a sinister force of undifferentiated individuals (SC, 1981). Such productions at least recognised that something of the shine is knocked off the miraculous Agincourt victory if it is achieved against merely posturing fools. Strutting braggarts are, after all, featured as much on the English side as on the French. The French, with the notable exception of the Dauphin, recognise Henry as a formidable opponent 'bred out of that bloody strain/That haunted us in our familiar paths' (II.iv.51–2). All of Henry's impressive performance in I.ii has been reported by the French ambassadors, as the Constable indicates by reference to his 'great state', 'noble counsellors', 'modesty' and 'constant resolution'. The French king fears that Henry will, as his English nobles advised (I.ii.114), emulate the 'warlike spirit' of the Black Prince (II.iv.48–64). Though critics have often downplayed the connections between Henry and Hal Shakespeare once again reminds us of it, as he has in every scene of the first two acts. If we summarise the passages that directly evoke the old Hal or register the effect of his transformation on others we see how frequent they are: I.i.22–69 (47), I.ii.245–99 (55), II.i.79–86 (8), 114–26 (13), II.ii.12–76 (65), II.iii.1–44 (44), II.iv.23–42 (20), 115–39 (25) – a total of 277 lines of the 1,013 lines of the first two acts, or 27.3 per cent. Canterbury, Ely, Nym and Pistol seem to believe the change in Henry to be genuine. The Dauphin appears to be unconvinced by Henry's transformation. The shrewd Constable of France, like Warwick before him (2 Henry IV, IV.iv.68–78), indicates that the political strategy behind the deliberate staging of the metamorphosis has not fooled him:

... you shall find his vanities forespent
Were but the outside of the Roman Brutus,
Covering discretion with a coat of folly,
As gardeners do with ordure hide those roots
That shall first spring and be most delicate.

                                    (II.iv.36–40)

This is language very much like that of Hal when he outlined his
strategy at the beginning of his career. The Dauphin's error in
viewing Henry as 'vain, giddy, shallow' (28) will prove as costly to
France as it did to Hotspur.

The scene is in two parts, with news of Henry being augmented
by Exeter's threats. The two parts are linked by a recall of English
triumphs at Crécy and Poitiers (II.iv.9–14, 48–64). Exeter uses
Edward III, father of the Black Prince, as the basis of Henry's
claim to the French throne and promises, if this claim is denied,
that the French will be held responsible before God for bringing
calamity on their own heads (II.iv.97–110), yet one more instance
of Henry's transference of guilt to others for the threatened
ravages of war. The references to God are frequent among the
English in contrast to the French who, if not exactly pagans, are
not noted for piety. There are ten references in I.ii to God (nine by
Henry, one by Canterbury) and nine in II.ii (four by Henry, and
four by his advisers). In the first French scene there are four
references to God, only one by Charles VI, the others by Exeter,
Henry's spokesman. Despite all their anxieties about war the
French rarely invoke the guidance or protection of God and rely
instead on their chivalric bravado.

The Chorus to Act III, in its vivid evocation of the channel
crossing and of an England left deserted by its 'choice drawn
cavaliers', launches the campaign. It supplies much of the heady
atmosphere of recruiting parades at war's outset. In one recent
production (SO, 1989) brass bands, Union Jacks and music-hall
songs reflected its World War One setting, a war fever soon to give
place to disillusion in the mud of France. The speech races forward
to the cannons 'With fatal mouths gaping on girded Harfleur' (27).
The French response to English demands is merely glanced at
(28–32) and given little weight in the urgency of the siege.

In the account of the Chorus there is no note of discord, faint-heartedness, or anything less than unstinted effort. We cannot avoid noticing that this is not an accurate depiction of what we see in Act III. Of the 226 lines of the ensuing three scenes, the 34 lines (15.0 per cent) of III.i fill out the picture the Chorus gives, the 134 lines (59.3 per cent) of III.ii contradicts it, and the 58 lines (25.7 per cent) of III.iii may at best be termed ambiguous support for the assault the Chorus implies was an irresistible triumph in its claim 'down all before them goes' (34). No matter how often the Chorus urges us to use our imaginations to re-create the glory, Shakespeare uses his imagination to call it into question. The Chorus's words throughout alert us to the manipulation of images which are as natural to the Chorus as effective role-playing is to Henry: *Chorus I*, 'invention', 'imaginary forces' (18), 'imaginary puissance' (25), 'Think ... that you see them' (26); *Chorus III*, 'imagin'd' (1), 'suppose' (3), 'play with your fancies' (7), 'do but think' (13), 'Work, work your thoughts' (25), 'Suppose' (27), 'eke out our performance with your mind' (35); *Chorus IV*, 'entertain' (1), 'Minding true things by what their mock'ries be' (52); *Chorus V*, 'Heave him away upon your winged thoughts' (8), 'in the quick forge and working house of thought' (23). The winged thoughts of the Chorus give us a heady survey of the heights but overlook many low spots. The juxtaposition of Chorus vision and Shakespeare vision is faintly reminiscent of the contradiction between the official account on Chinese television of the heroic army suppression of counter-revolution in Tiananmen Square in 1989 and the account foreign correspondents gave of the confused and brutal massacre of Beijing's student protesters. In this play we have to estimate whether, in terms of hard reality, what the Chorus makes in 'the quick forge of thought' is not so much horseshoes for proudly printing hoofs but something rather more like counterfeit money.

Those who see the play as a patriotic aria regard Henry's famous speech 'Once more unto the breach' in III.i as a high C. The power of rhetoric is under close examination in the play. It is not surprising that these ringing apostrophes are the best known elements of the play for they are so tactically placed and so carefully constructed by Henry to be memorable. Their potency has worked for centuries. Olivier made recruiting speeches for the WRNS in the Second World War, which, he records,

> always and without fail ended with 'Once more unto the breach'. The applause with which this was received helped me, and the audience, to feel that the whole discourse had been a success. (Olivier, 1982, p. 97)

In his film he reversed the usual method of dealing with monologues by starting out quietly in close-up, gradually widening the angle to a craning, high-angled shot of him with rising voice, curvetting on his white charger, building to a thunderous, stirring shout. The sequence emphasised his capacity to draw his men, through his charisma, into a compact unity. The confident assertion of the Chorus 'down goes all before them' is, however, evidently in dispute here for the king is trying to rally discouraged troops *retreating* from the breach. At III.ii.57–60 we find that some of the soldiers have had more than enough of the breach and that the sappers' attempts to mine the walls have been stymied by French countermines. This rallying cry does live up to the image promised at the outset of 'the warlike Harry' who can 'Assume the part of Mars' but in III.iii Henry is still outside Harfleur demanding that the gates be opened, which makes it clear that no breach sufficient to permit invasion has been made.

Henry addresses his soldiers as 'dear friends' and asks of them behaviour at which he is expert, acting, when he urges them to 'imitate the action of a tiger'. This implies, as was historically the case, and as Henry soon asserts (III.iii.56), that his army, depleted by sickness, is deeply discouraged. Henry works on various components – sinews, blood, brow, teeth, nostrils, breath, spirit – to give his men backbone and get them back in working order (III.i.6–17). There is something almost grotesque about this process of trying to transform his men into fierce beasts. What is miraculous about Agincourt is that it salvaged a campaign that was going badly by snatching victory from the very jaws of what looked like certain defeat. In blocking off a safe retreat to Calais the French imposed on the English a battle they had neither planned for nor wanted, as Henry clearly acknowledges (III.vi.148–64). Several recent productions have shown the English in disarray at this point. Langham (SO, 1966) had the opening lines delivered offstage, and the speech was something desperately improvised to rally exhausted troops. One critic noted of Ian Holm's Henry (SE, 1964) that he did not simply avoid heroics but 'was too hopelessly battle weary for heroics to be possible'. In the BBC TV production the speech met with groans and resistance from tired, disgruntled troops and Henry won them over only slowly with humorous challenges to their manhood. Branagh (SE, 1984) delivered it from a ladder with a ripely overblown urgency that suggested the audience view it as jingoistic blather. In an even more non-traditional view (SO, 1989) the speech was delivered to exhausted, shell-shocked troops, terrified by their experiences, one soldier screaming uncontrollably. The king strove in his speech to calm this one soldier's hysteria as if certain that only thus could he stem the retreat. The soldiers in these productions were far different from the temporarily repulsed force Olivier inspired astride his white charger and swinging his sword. These were armies already entertaining serious doubts about why they were stumbling around in the mud of France. An audience is now less likely to feel, buttons bursting with pride, how wonderful it is to be a sturdy bulldog of the island race. Nowadays we often see how the rhetoric of patriotism is shaped to whip men up to return to dangers that moments before they had fled from in terror.

This speech is inevitably related to another high C in the later battle, the Crispin Day speech (IV.iii.18–67). Alan Howard (SE, 1975) thought this first speech closer to conventional, tub-thumping, battle rhetoric, a sign that Henry was still somewhat distant from his men, hectoring them as a leader rather than approaching them as a fellow soldier. He saw, in the intimacy of the later speech, with its assertions of brotherhood, something that is lacking at Harfleur, and is the fruit of Henry's growing sense of identity with the desperate plight of his men, the ability to forge his army into a unit, which makes the difference at Agincourt. There is solid evidence in the speeches that an actor can use the first one as a stepping-stone to the second. In III.i, distinct hierarchical divisions in the army are appealed to separately and in different ways. The appeal to the 'noblest English' (17–25) emphasises the blood-lines stemming from renowned fathers. This relates again, as in I.ii and II.iv, to the storied deeds of their ancestors at Crécy and Poitiers where the English were so dominant there was action for only half the army, a distinct contrast to their current experience. Henry asserts that the nobility have set an example of how to fight 'to men of grosser blood', the inferior orders whose timorous nature, he may be implying, has caused this retreat. The yeomen he next addresses (III.i.25–30), technically freeholders below the rank of gentlemen, are commoners and countrymen, who include the archers who are to be a critical factor at Agincourt. The associations here are less of blood as of impressive physiques, 'limbs', the quality of which are related to 'pasture', a strength they develop, Henry implies, by breeding the sturdy cattle of England's shires. He asserts that they look noble (29–30), not quite the same as being noble, but a step on the way to the more democratic levelling of the Crispin Day speech. He joins together the two separate groups, nobles and yeoman, as greyhounds coupled on specially designed leashes for easy simultaneous release. Yet even as an army of distinct classes they are quite different from the French who, with their repeated sonorous roll-calls of aristocratic names, are infatuated with chivalric nobility to the exclusion of all consideration of the commoner. Their growing arrogance is based on contempt for an English army filled with common soldiers scarcely worthy enough to be fought by men of such mighty lineage and name. Yet Henry's phrase 'The game's afoot' implies the class-privileged view in which gentlemen can gain honour. It is a view which persists on the French side but disappears among the English as all ranks confront the muddy, unglamorous process of being ground down into 'warriors for the working day' in a campaign they seem progressively to be losing.

In response to Henry's stirring appeal we are not given, as we might expect, a sequence of vigorous battle episodes. Shakespeare instead, in III.ii, lingers over a hiatus in fighting which looks very much like deliberate bathos. That Nym and Pistol are not eager to go once more unto the breach is no surprise but Shakespeare did not need to show us their prudent resistance to the clarion call nor to have Bardolph parody it. They even have time to share a song, though it is cut in most productions. The Boy's wish to be safe with a drink in a London alehouse, which Pistol shares, reminds us that imitating the action of a tiger is not to everyone's taste. Only when their fears of Fluellen's blows are greater than their terror of the enemy are they induced to move. The placing at this point of the Boy's soliloquy, a speech almost as long as that of the Chorus, may seem odd in view of the urgency of the battle. It gives us a version of the campaign quite different from the official one. The Boy, the page Hal gave to Falstaff in the previous play, describes his criminal elders from Eastcheap sucking like horse-leeches persistently but with little success in France. Sometimes on stage they are shown at the outset of this scene filching the possessions of their dead battle comrades (SO, 1966, 1989). Compulsively they steal worthless things such as a lute-case and a fire-shovel in desperate pursuit of gain (38–40). This sequence prepares us for the execution of Bardolph and Nym for theft and for Pistol's preying on Le Fer at Agincourt. The Boy regards it as beneath his manhood to be corrupted and inducted into this brotherhood of thieves, a hope for an England less obsessively self-interested than in the past, but one that is dashed by his death at Agincourt.

Fluellen tries to beat the laggards towards the breach but does not himself stay there. When Gower summons him to attend the Duke of Gloucester at the mines he does not respond, resisting on principle rather than from a reluctance to fight. Like some of the military specialists of the time he believes the new-fangled reliance on gunpowder is a betrayal of the 'true disciplines' of the 'aunchiant wars'. He is an obsessive figure with a bee in his bonnet which drives every other consideration out of his mind. Macmorris considers it absurd to dispute with Fluellen about the 'Roman disciplines' when there is so much to be done (III.ii.99–107). In Terry Hands's production (SE, 1975), the captains did not play their scene as amiable comedy but were figures dangerously out of control, the kind of men who could go on the rampage in the way Henry threatens in the ensuing scene. Despite Macmorris's anger about ineffectual mining strategies and inactivity, an army regular's typical complaint about incompetent superiors, he does not *do* anything. Captain Jamy expects to do good service before the day is out even if it costs him his life (III.ii.108–10), but at the moment he wants to hear the debate between Fluellen and Macmorris. Following the most famous battle speech on record we see eight soldiers who avoid urgent action or engage in unprofitable debate and insults. Some are very belligerent, against each other rather than the French, and the evidence indicates that in this engagement Fluellen and Macmorris are no more effective than Pistol and Nym. Shakespeare presses on us the inescapable truth that when someone asserts 'The game's afoot' there are many who, for various reasons, are preoccupied with their own concerns.

A number of critics have considered this scene as possibly a late addition to the play, substitute material to replace, in a supposed earlier version such critics invent, the participation of Falstaff in the war (Walter, 1954, pp. xxxvi–xl). This seems improbable, however, if we consider how it develops central preoccupations, the juxtaposition of personal ambitions and needs with public duty and England's good, that is the spine of the whole tetralogy. Richard II set the struggle in motion by using his regal power to snatch Bolingbroke's inheritance to finance or make up for his own wasteful self-indulgence. In return Bolingbroke took the crown, satisfying his own personal ambition while striving to appear to be serving England's good. Rebels, in pursuit of personal power, proposed alternative candidates for the usurper's crown and, in the struggle, Hotspur, in singular pursuit of personal honour, and Falstaff, in pursuit of profit, were sacrificed. In this play we have to consider whether Henry's conquest is a hunger for territorial ambition or pursued for England's right and ultimate good. Henry believes he is sacrificing himself to the burden of leadership as he defined it to his father (*2 Henry IV*, IV.v.21–47, 158–77) and of which he will speak bitterly again on the eve of Agincourt.

The spasmodic dissension in the lower ranks is a much less significant threat to Henry than that of the rebels who ravaged his father's realm. We have a variety of figures who cannot always bring their personal needs into conformity with the demands of the army – a boy disgusted with his companions, soldiers avoiding the front line pursuing criminal profit, captains fuming in frustration, fussing about military rules, suspicious of their superiors.

Pistol can assert that 'God's vassals drop and die' (III.ii.7) but it is clear that neither he nor his mates want to be among them because they are frail men, 'men of mould' (III.ii.21) as Pistol phrases it to Fluellen. Fluellen's service at the mines is less important than his need to display his obsession with the 'disciplines of war', his Welshness, and his sense of dignity. We get a more immediate sense of history when these diverse figures are written in to augment the chronicles which ignore them and the Chorus which edits them out by taking note only of 'youths on fire' who are 'ciphers to this great accompt'. Amid danger and discouragement they are stubborn testimony to the persistence of individual vitality. Alan Howard has noted how well this scene fitted into the campaign as a stuttering sequence of actions constantly interrupted and halted by Falstaff's illness, the traitors, Falstaff's death, the French, the recoil from the breach, the captains' quarrels, Harfleur's capitulation followed by the retreat towards Calais, a relentless pattern that goes on and on (Beauman, 1976, p. 55). Shakespeare is not asserting that Henry has an inadequate army to wage his campaign; rather he is making it clear what armies are like. Henry persists with an army in which some are idle, some loyal, some thieves, some heroic, and some strutting clowns because his education has prepared him not to be surprised or disillusioned by it. Seeming to be what he is not is second nature to Henry and pretending his army is more potent than it is, as he does in III.iii, is an extension of that skill.

The language of the play expresses the waste and terror of war throughout. There are recurring images of the violation of women, echoed also in the way cities are talked of as women to be breached, of women widowed, children orphaned, the old left unsupported, the whole civilian population plundered by the rapacity of military campaigns. I have examined elsewhere how images of violence are spread across 650 lines (20.4 per cent) of the play (Brennan, 1989, pp. 199–203). Henry's threat to the citizens of Harfleur, III.iii.1–43, is the most concentrated account of this devastation not only in this play but in Shakespeare's entire canon. In his Arden edition Walter (1954, p. 66) asserts that this does not reflect any discredit on Henry for it is simply part of the military protocol of the day. John Dover Wilson, in his Cambridge edition

(1947, p. 150), cites a law in Deuteronomy to defend Henry's threats. Sherman Hawkins (1975, p. 341) believes that at Harfleur Henry shows exemplary virtues, fortitude in assaulting it and temperance in sparing its inhabitants. In an article published not long after the Boer War Sidney Lee convinced himself the French had only themselves to blame for these threats:

> It is only when a defeated enemy declines to acknowledge the obvious ruins of his fortune that a sane and practical patriotism defends resort on the part of the conquerer to the grimmest measure of severity. The healthy instinct stiffens the grip on the justly won fruits of victory. (Lee, 1906, p. 176)

It has been noted that it is ludicrous to defend Henry by reference to medieval treatises on the proprieties of war when Shakespeare so vividly gives us a picture of how war, despite all references to God, justice, mercy and the rules of war, is a massive assault on the foundations of civilisation (Ornstein, 1972, p. 191).

Henry's speech juxtaposes 'your people ... my soldiers', defenceless civilians and marauding army. He strings together a sequence of words to create a tidal wave of blood and disaster hanging over Harfleur: 'destruction ... batt'ry ... ashes ... fleshed ... bloody hand ... wide as hell, mowing like grass ... impious war ... prince of fiends ... smirched ... fell feats ... licentious wickedness ... fierce career ... enrag'd soldiers in their spoil ... leviathan ... filthy and contagious clouds/Of heady murder, spoil, and villainy' (III.iii.4–31). Whereas the army is associated with hell and filth as a pestilence, the citizens are seen as clean, 'Your fresh fair virgins', 'flow'ring infants', and yet inviting rape by their purity:

> What is't to me, when you yourselves are cause,
> If your pure maidens fall into the hand
> Of hot and forcing violation?
>                              (III.iii.18–20)

The speech reaches its climax when these two elements are mingled together in a passage which recalls paintings of the rape of the Sabine women or the Massacre of the Innocents:

. . . in a moment look to see
The blind and bloody soldier with foul hand
Defile the locks of your shrill-shrieking daughters;
Your fathers taken by their silver beards.
And their most reverend heads dash'd to the walls;
Your naked infants spitted upon pikes,
Whiles the mad mothers with their howls confus'd
Do break the clouds, as did the wives of Jewry
At Herod's bloody-hunting slaughtermen.

(III.iii.33–41)

This is a picture of an army rather different from the 'choice-drawn cavaliers' promoted by the Chorus. Henry's images remind one of Tamburlaine's threats before Damascus and are as revolting as anything Goya presented in *Los Desastres de la Guerra*. Henry's Pilate-like washing of his hands at such atrocities is disturbing. As Kernan (1970, p. 270) notes, who on earth does he think brought this gang to France? Here Shakespeare is bringing out 'certain contradictions, human and moral, which seem to be inherent in the notion of a successful king' (Traversi, 1956, p. 41).

This speech is not based on any of the chronicle sources. In Holinshed there are protracted negotiations which involved the yielding of hostages and messages back and forth to the French king until Harfleur yielded, after which 'the towne was sacked, to the great gaine of the Englishmen' (Bullough, 1962, p. 338). This last detail is historically incorrect although Henry did take its leading citizens prisoner and evicted many of its inhabitants. Shakespeare simplifies this lengthy process. Because Harfleur does not get the relief it expects from the Dauphin, Henry is able to frighten it into submission and then instruct Exeter to 'Use mercy to them all' (III.iii.54). In order to protect Henry against the imputation of savagery, productions, even recent ones, have usually made heavy cuts in the speech, a result, perhaps, of the fact that we often think that passing on responsibility for atrocities to the victims is more typical of sadistic torturers in repressive police states. The Olivier film cut all of the threats. Half or more of Henry's speech has often been excised (SE, 1943, 1946, 1951, 1964, 1984; SO, 1956, 1966; BBC TV). Only one of the productions of the

last sixty years I have examined presented the scene uncut. Alan
Howard (SE, 1975) gave the speech with great sternness, but he
almost vomited after completing the threats and collapsed with
emotional relief when the Governor yielded the town. It was
presented as a gambling bluff, an attempt to force a submission he
was not sure he could achieve by military means. The justification
for this approach is Henry's remark to Exeter:

> For us, dear uncle,
> The winter coming on, and sickness growing
> Upon our soldiers, we will retire to Calais.
>
> (III.iii.54–6)

In this admission, as one critic has noted, Henry for the first time
puts rhetoric aside and begins to talk like an honest man (Babula,
1977, p. 53), a contrast all the more effective in that it comes immediately after his thunderous performance as War and Rapine. In his
army, riddled with dysentery and fever at this siege, some two thousand died and as many as five thousand may have had to be sent
back to England. A reading of his threat as a calculated bluff to spare
a dwindling army, not eager to fight, from combat is plausible. We
can only fully understand it as such at the end of the scene for we
are hoodwinked along with the citizens of Harfleur. This effect is
often undone on stage by having the Governor and citizens of
Harfleur on the battlements visibly quailing at the threats. As Gary
Taylor in his Oxford edition (1982, p. 50) points out, this assures
the audience that the French will submit. By delaying the
Governor's entrance until Henry's threat is completed, Shakespeare clearly intends to focus our minds on the terror of Henry's
ultimatum and to leave us in tense uncertainty about whether it will
succeed or whether he will have to fulfil his savage promises.
Because we are no longer insiders, as we were with Hal, we cannot
be certain how far Henry will go. Only in his instructions to Exeter
can we see that he has staged himself in another of his successful performances. Michael Pennington (ESC, 1986) whistled to
himself at the Governor's submission, relieved that he had brought
off his bluff. Alan Howard (SE, 1975), in his oscillation from
belligerence to tearful relief, prepared for the increasingly desperate
situation of the English in subsequent scenes.

Shakespeare now introduces what one critic terms the most abrupt peripeteia he ever wrote, rather as if a Gilbert and Sullivan song were inserted in the last act of *Tristan and Isolde* (Hammond, 1987, p. 140), the charming innocence of Princess Katharine's English lesson. The scene, from which nowadays a line is scarcely ever cut, was omitted from virtually all productions until the late nineteenth century. The functions which it performs were not recognised. In a play in which women speak less than 5 per cent of the lines this scene deftly reminds us what is missing from this unnatural world of military strife. Its effect is doubled by having it follow the play's most violent speech evoking the brutality of rape. Because we know that Henry will marry Katharine her struggle to learn English seems to be the pursuit of a fruitful path in contrast to the destructive carnage in which the men are engaged. It is a scene often set amid flowers (BBC TV) or espaliered trees (Olivier's film) to emphasise orderly cultivation. Guthrie, at the Old Vic in 1937, raised the women on a palanquin, and the Branagh film cleverly had the princess deliver the complete list of sexually suggestive English words from within a curtained four-poster bed. Terry Hands's staging (SE, 1975) was a dazzling realisation of Shakespeare's intent. As the ramp which was used for the assault on Harfleur was lowered, the women appeared at the rear in the dispersing smoke of battle, like an apparition, confronting Henry almost as a prophetic dream of the better world he would reach at the conclusion of his journey.

In this scene, as often elsewhere in the play, there is a focus on impediments to communication. Canterbury's claim that the Salic law is 'as clear as is the summer's sun' (1.ii.86) expresses a confidence that few are likely to share. Nym and Pistol employ blustering, overblown insults to conceal their timidity. We must work through the Hostess's laughable malapropisms to grasp the genuine nature of her grief. Fluellen and Macmorris, in juxtaposed accents, issue mannered threats which are elaborate ways of saying very little. The chief charm of this language lesson is the way the innocent women, without at first being aware of it, stumble on obscenities in the way they pronounce the English equivalents for French words. 'Bilbow' (26) the English audience might relate to the flexible and phallic bilbao sword. Katharine pronounces 'neck' as 'nick', often a slang term for vulva, as her later distortion 'ilbow' (43) may be. For 'chin' she says 'sin' (33), pronounces 'nails' as 'mails', and uses the French word 'robe' (46) which can be related to 'bonas robas', English slang for 'loose women'. She only notices the double meanings when told the English word for 'pied' is 'foot' (47), which relates to the French word 'foutre', and when Alice gives 'count', her mispronunciation of 'gown', as the English equivalent of 'robe', the word 'count' also having, for Katharine, immodest implications because of its closeness in sound to a French sexual word. Given this kind of context 'hand' and 'finger' get drawn into the network of suggestiveness so that her recitation of the whole list of words she has learnt (53–5) implies a progression of approaches up the arm to the face and then down to more central sexual targets. Katharine considers the words 'gros et impudique' and not to be used by ladies chary of their honour, but nevertheless proceeds to use them three times, almost invariably spoken on stage with a clear hint of sexual excitement, which anticipates the wooing of the play's close.

The French in III.v are convinced that English success stems not from any innate merit but from their own neglect. Henry's success is even more difficult to accept because 'his numbers are so few,/His soldiers sick and famished in their march' (III.v.56–7). The Constable assumes he will be cheated of a fight worthy of his honour and that Henry will ask for ransom to avoid a fight (55–60), a recurrent refrain of the French until they lose the battle.

The audience is surprised in III.vi to hear from Fluellen of Pistol's bravery, no doubt a strutting pretence of valour which hoodwinks the French as it later does Le Fer. Pistol's old-fashioned vaunting probably takes in Fluellen because it fits his archaic view of the disciplines of war. The Frenchmen in the previous scene have undervalued the English and now Fluellen, an experienced veteran, overvalues one of them, though Pistol soon betrays his true worth when he tries to bribe Fluellen and exploit the impression he has made on him to extract a favour. Pistol babbles on at length about Bardolph as a victim of 'giddy Fortune's furious fickle wheel' (III.vi.24–8), only to be interrupted by Fluellen, who is not about to put up with a lot of hot air on such a topic when he can pour more of it out himself (29–37). No matter how minor Pistol claims Bardolph's crime to be Fluellen will not violate the disciplines of war. After Pistol's departure Gower, in a long speech (66–79), usually cut on stage, indicates how the rogue, once back in London's taverns, will pretend to heroism, a shrewd recognition of how fantasy reinvents the glamour of war. That Gower, not the brightest of intellects, can see through Pistol tells us something about Fluellen's limitations. Gower's advice to Fluellen not to be taken in is Shakespeare's implicit corrective for the audience, perhaps, to the version the Chorus presents, 'But you must learn to know such slanders of the age or else you may be marvellously mistook' (III.vi.77–9).

The Boy's soliloquy in III.ii informs us of the criminal activity of his companions. The chronicles contain a widely noted instance of Henry's exemplary punishment of a thieving soldier and Shakespeare uses it to finish off Bardolph. In the chronicles the condemned soldier stole a pyx, a box containing the consecrated wafers for communion, and is reported to have eaten the hosts it contained. This is more valuable than the pax Shakespeare has Bardolph steal, a tablet stamped with a crucifix kissed by communicants, often of gilded copper, which the rogue may have mistaken for gold. The punishment for what Pistol calls 'pax of little price' must, therefore, seem much more severe than it is in Shakespeare's source. Pistol, a thief himself, certainly views it as unnecessarily severe. Fluellen's view that it is necessary is clearly no guide given what we know about his fanaticism concerning rules. By making Bardolph the victim Shakespeare complicates the issue of Henry as a stern disciplinarian which is emphasised in the sources. One production ducked the issue altogether by leaving out Bardolph's name so that the punished figure was the anonymous soldier of the sources (SO, 1956). One critic has suggested that this moment strips the king not only of personal friends but also of a private past so that for Henry to recognise Bardolph, let alone to regret him, is impossible (Barton, 1975, p. 105).

Directors have certainly not followed that line of reasoning in recent productions, but have fastened on this moment as a turning-point in Henry's experience. Alan Howard (SE, 1975) paused on learning the thief was Bardolph to indicate that all of his past with the Eastcheap rogues flashed through his mind, before signalling his consent to Exeter for the execution. As it took place offstage Pistol stared Henry straight in the eye. Even though Henry was committed to being seen to do the right thing the execution evidently shook him deeply. It poignantly recalled a moment in *1 Henry IV* (II.iv.316) when Hands had Henry hang Bardolph in mocking mime in a scarf at the line 'No, if rightly taken, halter', thus prophesying from the meteors and exhalations on Bardolph's face, which Fluellen has just used to identify the thief, his ultimate fate. That expert in long-range planning anticipates this moment just as he foresees Falstaff's banishment in the same scene. Hands followed the text by not executing Bardolph on stage, but other directors have striven to press the horror of the moment more forcibly on an audience. Langham (SO, 1966) had Bardolph's body, his throat bloodied by the hangman's rope, brought onstage and dumped at the king's feet. Adrian Noble (SE, 1984) made an unforgettably chilling moment of it with the soldiers, crouching under tarpaulins in a steady rain, being given an example of summary justice as a deterrent against pillaging. Henry (Kenneth Branagh), a battle veteran of sudden angers as well as cold-blooded decisions, watched the execution on stage. Bardolph, old and helpless, was made to kneel in front of the beefy Exeter. Henry, remembering the past friendship, steeled himself to his duty and, at his nod, Exeter strangled the condemned man and, with a final jerk, snapped his neck. Henry turned away, almost collapsed in sick horror, and had to be supported. In his film this moment is even more heavily emphasised by Branagh and given a proportional weight well beyond anything in the text. When the king consents to the hanging of Bardolph from a tree-bough there is a flashback to the merriment of the Eastcheap tavern. The cart on which Bardolph stands is driven away and he hangs, his legs pumping in jerky spasms. The swinging corpse is visible during the French herald's demands, the army exits under the body, and the Chorus prefaces the following scene with it still in view. These directors evidently want to make the point that, though Henry may shift responsibility for the violent consequences of his actions to others whenever possible, in this case he has to accept the disturbing task as unmistakably his. It is worth noting that if Henry does experience any pain Shakespeare does not show it in his lines. The fact that Henry issues a reflex response about the need for discipline is, perhaps, more chilling and more telling on an audience than a director's ingenious embroidery of the incident to press its significance on us. It is a moment which allows Henry to signal very clearly once again 'Presume not that I am the thing I was'.

In the three part arrangement of the scene, with its brief central passage of the execution, there is an ironic relationship between the opening and closing. Fluellen tells Pistol that he is a man so committed to discipline that he would not intercede for Bardolph even if 'he were my brother'. In the execution it is clear that Henry, like Fluellen, will not consider clemency even for an old friend. In the final segment of the scene Mountjoy, speaking for the French king, treats Henry as a criminal he has not yet troubled to punish. Henry has stolen Harfleur but is offered, as Bardolph is not, a second chance of desisting from further theft if he pays a compensatory ransom to avoid the full punishment he would receive in battle. Mountjoy asserts he 'hath betrayed his followers whose condemnation is pronounced' (III.vi.129–30). The issue of Henry's responsibility for his men's lives, resulting from the debatable justice of his cause, will soon be placed squarely in front of him by his own soldiers on the eve of Agincourt.

It begins to seem that the French confidence in victory, despite the loss of Harfleur, is not misplaced. Henry at this point, the chronicles record, offered to lessen his claims and pay for damages in exchange for unmolested passage to Calais, a detail Shakespeare blurs. Though he admits it is not wisdom to do so Henry, who at line 85 of the Folio enters with his 'poore soldiers', refers to the frail, vulnerable state of his army again and again III.vi.135–7, 140–2, 149–50, 159–60). Henry moves in the play into a steadily closer sense of identity with his soldiers. At Agincourt he puts his experiences as Prince Hal among the commoners to work for him. He had anticipated this moment early in his career:

I am sworn brother to leash of drawers and can tell them all by their christen names . . . and when I am King of England I shall command all the good lads of Eastcheap.

(*1 Henry IV*, II.iv.6–14)

There was in him some contempt for the 'drawers' and 'under-skinkers' he could so easily take in with his pretence of brother-hood and, as we are later made aware, that private disdain persists. Henry, however, unlike either his father or Richard II, has the acting skills to make the role of plain, blunt, unpretentious 'lad of mettle' work among his soldiers. He asserts that he will not yield the ransom Mountjoy demands to exploit the usual loophole that allowed a king and his noblemen to escape the consequences of pursuing an ill-judged battle. His only hope for success is to inspire his soldiers to an extraordinary effort against uneven odds. To weld them into an effective unit he must become one of them and risk his life, without hope of ransom, as they are doing. It is with the French herald he begins to shape the image of himself, which develops scene by scene, as ordinary workaday warrior.

In III.vii we have the longest scene of the four devoted exclusively to the French before battle, and the one which defines them in the least flattering way, coming as it does in immediate contrast to Henry's performance as unpretentious warrior, a contrast stage décor often emphasises. In Olivier's film the French are in gaudy new uniforms at their ease in a well-appointed pavilion, as they are in the BBC production at a table filled with exotic fruits on expensive silverware. They are often given golden armour to make them seem deliberately archaic, living beyond their time into an earthier, less glamorous age (SE, 1975). In Noble's production (SE, 1984) they were set lounging at their ease some distance apart, athletes awaiting a sporting amusement, speaking out to the audience rather than to each other to emphasise their insular arrogance. Such relaxed luxury contrasts with the English camp where drab, muddy, scarecrow figures huddle together for warmth. We never see anything of the French lower orders but their high-command is not the co-operative brotherhood Henry forges in his army. The French scarcely consider death, which is an obsessive concern among the English, but prefer to talk competitively about their armour, their horses and the number of prisoners they will take. The Dauphin's lines are, in the quarto, given to Bourbon and his presence at Agincourt is unhistorical but Shakespeare, to set off Henry, shows the man, who had mocked the English king for immaturity, to be an absurd braggart stuffed with juvenile enthusiasms. The scene is shot through with urgent exclamations of yearning to display their skills, 'Will it never be day?' on nine occasions (lines 2, 6, 11, 78, 81, 88, 89, 127, 152), mingled with an awareness of how the English must be dreading the dawn (III.vii.127–36). Because of our foreknowledge of the outcome the scene is coloured with a rich irony. In contrast to the English, asking for God's aid, desiring to meet death with a clear conscience, the French neither mention God nor give considera-tion to the state of their souls. Productions have frequently striven to underline a decadence in the French camp; Charles Kean and other directors in the nineteenth century, taking their cue from the Chorus, often presented the French at dice, Benson had dancing girls available, and a recent production (SO, 1989) set this scene in a brothel with the generals drunk, pants around their ankles, in a kind of sexual heat for battle. One critic finds in them a resurrec-tion of old defeated impulses strong earlier in the tetralogy in the isolated egotism and arrogant bravado of Hotspur and Falstaff (Allman, 1980, p. 112). We register an irony in the obsessive pride with which they boast about their horses (III.vii.1-68, 75–81) which we know will soon lead them to their deaths. Instead of having in a few hours, as Orleans boasts, 'each a hundred English-men' (153), the French deaths will outnumber the English, in Shakespeare's account, four hundred to one.

## · 3 ·

# 'A little touch of Harry in the night': The eve of battle

The prologue to the fourth act is the climactic example of the vivid scene-setting skills of the Chorus. It tells us, in its account of Henry's tour among his soldiers, how things could happen and, in terms of a national epic, how things ought to happen, but not of how, in fact, in Shakespeare's IV.i, they *do* happen. The whole speech has a clearly organised four part structure: *Part 1* (1–16), *Part 2* (17–28a), *Part 3* (28b-47), *Part 4* (48–53). In *Part 1* (1–16) the time is characterised in sights and sounds, 'creeping murmur' and 'poring dark'; noises uniting both armies, 'The hum', 'stilly sounds', 'secret whispers of each other's watch'. Details which catch the eye, 'fire', 'paly flames', 'umber'd face', mingle with further sounds, 'boastful neighs/Piercing night's dull ear', 'busy hammers closing rivets up'. Words which relate the armies mingle with the common sights and sounds, 'camp to camp', 'either army', 'fire answers fire', 'each battle', 'Steed threatens steed', as armourers work on the knights in both camps. There is brief reference to elements external to both camps, parts of an enduring landscape of peace, there before battle and, it is hoped, afterwards – the 'country cocks' crowing, the village 'clocks' tolling the hours across the flickering fields busy with activity. After the details that unite the camps *Part 2* (17–28a) juxtaposes elements which make the camps quite different; the 'over-lusty French', their confidence noted in the gambling at dice for their weakened foes, impatient to test their valour; the English transfixed by fear, like 'sacrifices' on the fiery altar of war, already looking like battle-dead, 'so many horrid ghosts' with 'gestures sad' and 'lank lean cheeks', wan and pallid beneath 'the gazing moon'. *Part 3* (28b-47) introduces the figure that more than compensates for the imbalance between the two sides, 'the royal captain of this ruined band'. Henry is first presented in motion 'walking from watch to watch' in contrast to his army sitting lost in fearful thoughts. He first greets these pale figures with the warmth of a 'modest smile' on his 'royal face' which registers no fear, nor any sign of fatigue from anxious watching. The 'little touch of Harry in the night' thaws 'cold fear', revives his men, dispels the pale moonlight to bring a new dawn of hope to his whole army. The passage confirms Henry's movement towards identity with his army when he 'calls them brothers, friends, and countrymen' and when his warmth works on 'mean and gentle all', references preparing the ground for the St Crispin's Day speech. We may recall again how Richard II emphasised his relation to Christ in terms of betrayal and death. Henry, by contrast, resurrects 'horrid ghosts' from death, a deliberate identification with the Saviour, one of an increasing number in this section of the play. In the ensuing scene, however, Shakespeare insists on showing us how Henry experiences his Gethsemane. In *Part 4* (48–53), after this spectacular evocation, we are reminded of the inadequacies of a stage which can only offer action unworthy of 'The name of Agincourt'. The Chorus disdains the 'vile and ragged foils,/Right ill-disposed in brawl ridiculous'. Shakespeare makes precisely such a brawl between Pistol and Le Fer, the broadest burlesque of heroic feats in the more-than-a-dozen battles in his plays, the most extended action of the various events he shows us at Agincourt. The dramatist presses on us the disgrace for which the Chorus apologises so that when we 'sit and see', we will indeed be 'Minding true things by what their mock'ries be' in a sense quite different from the one the Chorus intends.

   It is unfortunate that a speech of such masterful construction is, nowadays in the theatre, almost invariably cut up and distributed as narrative prefaces to various scenes, which completely dissipates the effect of its sweeping survey. Lines 1–22a are used as a preface to III.vii, while 22b-48 are retained in position here as prologue to IV.i, and 49–53 are either cut or slipped in just before the opening alarum of battle in IV.iv. This arrangement has, since the early 1960s, developed as a tradition and has been used in all but one of the last seven productions of the RSC and Stratford, Ontario Festival, as well as the Branagh film and the ESC production. Only the director who resists this barbarous practice of parcelling out the speech has a chance of achieving the effect at which Shakespeare aims of producing that momentous pause in the action, the midnight activity which plays upon our foreknowledge that subsequent events will not accord at all with the attitudes of overconfidence and fearful apprehension displayed in the two camps. Placed as a continuous sequence before IV.i it highlights the persuasive way in which the Chorus strives to win us towards its version. We have just witnessed the French noblemen in the previous scene and the account the Chorus offers is an accurate summary of our experience. We note, too, that for the first time the Chorus seems to allow some of the uncomfortable facts about the wretchedness of the English army to appear in its account. This is very different from the triumphant army embarking for battle (Chorus II) and eagerly falling on Harfleur (Chorus III). We have seen much that has conflicted with these accounts and can believe the 'poor condemned English' do need to be cheered up by their leader. In one account of Henry's life, there is an indication that he visited and encouraged his troops during the siege of Harfleur, but there is no mention of it in the chronicles Shakespeare knew. Because of the accuracy of its report on the French we may be prone to submit to the Chorus's account of this Christ-like visit of Harry glimmering as a light in a dark world. We are not at all prepared for what Shakespeare shows us in the subsequent scene. One production (SO, 1966) strove to ram home the contradiction by bringing on Henry, after this description of a saintly monarch, as being short-tempered, insecure and ravaged with anxiety about his chances. There is no need to load the evidence so heavily, for the play eloquently presents its own contradiction of the Chorus. Henry does not go as a king to inspire and cheer his men, but in disguise discovers their deep anxieties about the justice of his cause. At one point he argues so heatedly that he almost comes to blows with one of his soldiers. Far from inspiring his men he is, on the evidence of his soliloquy and prayer, dispirited and even angry at his experience among them. He is not united with them at this point as 'brothers, friends, and countrymen', but made only too painfully aware of how deeply he is separated from them. Because of his disguise the soldiers know nothing of this, but, as always, this role-playing provides Henry with information he can turn to his own advantage. He learns how important it is to assure his men that he is their brother. The Chorus asserts that Henry's leadership was natural, easy and spontaneous whereas Shakespeare indicates that it is learnt, which reinforces the essence of his interpretation of Henry throughout as a pragmatic politician. In well-tried theatre tradition the eve of Agincourt is the disastrous dress rehearsal which is fixed for the opening of the show – the St Crispin's Day battle speech.

The climax in *Henry V*, as in *Richard III*, is the night before battle. It is iv.i rather than the battle of Agincourt that is the pivotal sequence in the issue that has been developing through three plays, Henry's struggle with the role of kingship. The Chorus has told us how well Henry conceals fears of destruction which afflict his men. In his first line Henry admits 'we are in great danger', a peril he exploits to suggest 'There is some soul of goodness in things evil' (iv.i.4). The notion that every cloud has a silver lining is a notion we expect in a man who has spent his life structuring contrasts of bright metal on sullen ground. This scene will demand more expertise in gathering 'honey from the weed' (11) than he anticipates. The language associated with resurrection, prominent in the speech of the Chorus, continues in the language of the king (19–23). Bullough argues that Shakespeare may have adapted this scene from Tacitus' account of the tour Germanicus made among his troops. In that account there is only the general's overhearing of the high regard in which he is held by his soldiers and no direct conversation with them. It has been pointed out that in several plays by Shakespeare's contemporaries there is a king-in-disguise sequence which usually shows that, when a king and commoner can talk together informally, problems can be solved and grievances redressed. Shakespeare, however, uses this familiar device

> in order to question, not to celebrate, a folk convention . . . to summon up the memory of a wistful, naive attitude towards history and the relationship of subject and king which this play rejects as attractive but untrue: a nostalgic but false romanticism. (Barton, 1975, pp. 96–9)

In borrowing Erpingham's cloak Henry is prepared for the possibility of disguise, but it may be that his intention is to debate with his bosom awhile without interruption for, in the subsequent sequences, he does not seek out company. Pistol approaches and challenges him, he overhears Fluellen and Gower without attempting to interfere, and, with the other soldiers, he only engages in conversation when, like wary guards, they challenge him to unfold his identity. Henry will get to debate with his bosom but the apartness he seeks is pressed on him in a way he neither looks for nor wants. Henry is challenged by Pistol to identify himself as officer or one of the 'base, common, popular' (38), a distinction the subsequent argument and resulting soliloquy embroider at length. This is the only direct contact Henry has with the Eastcheap rogues. He calls himself Harry Leroy, not a Cornish name, as Pistol believes, but one of deeper significance than any Tom, Dick or Harry. It is what he claims to be and hopes to become, the king of France, an identity that, even in disguise, he cannot escape.

His concern for his common soldiers is one responsive to the precepts of books on military conduct, which advise especial concern at night. Books on government constantly advise rulers to find ways to discover the real opinions of their people. As an aid in disguise Shakespeare has Henry speak in prose. The issue of obedience, especially to orders that may be contrary to God's commandments, or about the justice of which there was uncertainty and ambiguity, was a matter of extensive debate in Shakespeare's time. That Shakespeare considered there was some question about the justice of Henry's cause can be seen from the extensive consideration given to it in i.ii and iv.i. In contemporary accounts the balance of opinion went in Henry's favour. Gentili's assertion that Henry's claim was 'not an empty one' was fastened on by Elizabethan militants, and Fulke Greville argued that war to enforce a legal claim was justifiable. But the heavy responsibility that war laid on a king, whose primary task was the welfare of his subjects, was not overlooked, especially when the cause was doubtful. As a contemporary theorist phrased it, 'If the unjustice of the warres be not notorious, the subject is bound to pay and serve and the guilte shall be laid to his charge that commandeth him to serve' (Jorgensen, 1956, p. 164). The first comment Henry hears about the signs of dawn is 'we have no great cause to desire the approach of day' (87–8), which prompts Williams to speculate that they are unlikely to see the end of it. When asked what his commander's opinion is of their position Henry can give little positive encouragement, 'Even as men wreck'd upon the sand, that look to be wash'd off the next tide' (97–8), which suggests they are unlikely to be saved by their own efforts. If Henry introduces this note of hopeless pessimism to draw out of his soldiers their deepest fears, he is certainly not disappointed.

The Chorus has presented us with a picture of communion conceived in almost religious terms. In the two bodies of kingship Henry has shared his 'modest smile', 'royal face', 'cheerful semblance', 'liberal eye', that 'little touch' of himself as though, among 'his host' he were himself the host or wafer of communion to bring life to the ghosts who surround him. In this scene the words 'God' and 'Christ' appear ten times, eight of them in Henry's speech, and there are many other words with religious implications: soul (five times), conscience (3), guilt/guilty (2), damnation (2), pardon (2), spirit, wickedness, sins, fault, heaven, the latter day, priest, preachers, penitence, chantries, contrite. In this scene, however, we are dealing mainly with the king's mortal body, an emphasis Henry himself makes: 'I think the king is but a man as I am: the violet smells to him as it doth to me . . . all his senses have but human condition; his ceremonies laid by, in his nakedness he appears but a man' (100–6). This scene, far from being the public communion the Chorus describes, is more like a trial or mortification of the flesh. It is so, of course, because Henry is the only king in the cycle who takes the trouble to discover the anxieties of his people. Henry VI may sit on a molehill and wish to be a shepherd when he observes the self-destruction of his people. Richard II may also declare, like Henry:

> I live with bread like you, feel want,
> Taste grief, need friends; subjected thus
> How can you say to me I am a king?
> (*Richard II*, iii.ii.175–7)

Yet despite that acknowledgement of his mortality Richard loses his crown because he believes his kingship not only separates him from his fellow men, but makes him invulnerable to them. He revises his view only when he has lost his crown, a mistake Henry avoids.

Henry's soldiers recognise that their situation is so dire that, as Bates says, the 'outward courage' of the king cannot disguise the fact that he must know he would be better off up to his neck in the Thames. It would be even better if he were here alone to yield for ransom and save many lives. Some critics believe that Henry wins the ensuing argument and exhibits the inspiring common touch of leadership. We are surely meant to notice that the argument Williams makes about the king's responsibility for his men's souls if his cause is not just ought to be familiar to Henry, for it is precisely the same argument he made to Canterbury at the out-set (i.ii.13–28). When it served his purpose at Harfleur Henry described war as a pestilence of murder and rapine visited on the innocent, whereas he now argues that it is God's beadle to purge the world of sinners. Henry himself, of course, may be one of those sinners to be purged. His dwindling army, his need to winter in Calais to recover strength, the overwhelming odds he faces in confronting the French army on the morrow might lead him to believe that God has not forgotten his father's usurpation of the crown. His soldiers apply his favourite tactic of laying responsi-bility for destruction of others on him and he strenuously resists. Williams fastens on the violence war visits on its victims, 'those legs and arms and heads chopp'd off' (135–6), 'the wives left poor behind', 'the children rawly left' (140–3). This is more of what Hamlet would consider bitter wormwood, for the sacrificial lambs Henry invoked at Harfleur are now laid crying at his door. The initial charge is that a monarch must be blamed for his soldiers' deaths 'if the cause be not good'. But eventually Williams holds the king responsible for any unshriven sins on his soldiers' souls if they die in battle. It is on this loophole that Henry fastens. Many critics indicate a dissatisfaction with Henry's response to the challenge put to him. Henry's answer is adequate to the final formulation proposed by Williams, for a king certainly cannot be held responsible for his soldiers' private crimes since 'every subject's soul is his own'. Henry makes his point with an overkill of examples which wins assent from his soldiers though it completely ignores the more serious charge in the argument. Henry sticks to the blanket definition of his culpability rather than the specific one because he knows, as the soldiers must know, that the cause of the son of a usurper is not as unambiguous as he would like to claim, since his pursuit of the French crown depends in the first place on whether his claim to the English crown is unshadowed by doubt. Henry makes clear his urgent need to avoid any connection between the actions and crimes of fathers and sons (iv.i.146–9). So his men do not get a magical 'little touch of Harry in the night' thawing their cold fears but rather 'a little touch of an anonymous subaltern who only succeeds in getting their backs up' (Arden, 1977, p. 203).

The king grows irritated because, under the successful disguise that deceives his men, he nevertheless discovers that they consider him to be an actor encouraging them to fight by assuring them that the king is willing to die with them though they are convinced Henry probably has no such intention. Even though they are willing to fight lustily for him they know that he has ways of protecting his vulnerability unavailable to them. Having led them to certain slaughter, they believe he will accept ransom, the well-tried escape route of the privileged. Henry vehemently asserts the king would never accept ransom and is mocked as a fool by Williams, a jibe that so riles him that they almost come to blows over the issue. Henry cannot take the advantage, so often enjoyed by Hal in exposing Falstaff's fantastic lies, of revealing his double role. He has to swallow his pride, accept the suspicions, and find some way of dealing with them.

Henry's rough handling in this debate leads to his only soliloquy in the play (iv.i.226–80), a speech of great importance because it gives us our only direct access to his thoughts unhindered by calculations about how much his words are shaped by his role-playing aims. Only about 2.5 per cent of the play is devoted to soliloquies, whereas in the *Henry VI* and *Henry IV* plays the percentage is always at least twice as high and in *Richard III* very much higher. The sparse use of soliloquy and asides in this play shapes our sense that the king is now very much a public figure. Given the perilous circumstances of his campaign, the increasing sickness of his army, Henry is remarkably discreet and reticent with the audience, especially in view of the fact that he speaks almost a third of the play's lines. In this angry, disillusioned outburst we discover the inner pressures we have felt building up behind his public rhetoric from the outset, the strain of having to shape everything for public consumption to compel conviction in the king's cause and integrity which he now discovers has been less than universally successful. As Kenneth Branagh notes, 'It is the confirmation that he will forever be utterly alone' (Jackson and Smallwood, 1988, p. 103). Some critics believe the speech reveals him to be simply not very interesting, devious without being complicated, a man whose 'mental and physical constitution is a mechanism for producing political results, not self-awareness' (Berry, 1980, p. 59). In a production it is sometimes given in calm reflection (SO, 1980, 1989; BBC TV; Olivier's film) or with weary resignation (SE, 1984). Christopher Plummer started it with bitter resentment (SO, 1956) and Alan Howard (SE, 1975) showed a great deal of agitation. Michael Pennington's debate with his soldiers (ESC, 1986) had been confidently patronising rather than desperate so the soliloquy began in irritation but slowly modulated to a kind of weary amusement.

This moment relates back to the time when Richard II, in his deposition scene, undoes himself, washes away ceremony until he is unkinged and merely a man. Henry is reminded of his mortality because his men are so clearly concerned about their own and believe he does not take the same risks as they do. His anger naturally enough rationalises his privilege so that he sees it not as a means of giving him greater freedom but as an inescapable burden that gives him less, which uncovers some less than admirable qualities in the king in his disdain for and envy of his subjects. In the view of one critic the speech asks us

> to accept the grotesque and cruelly unequal distribution of possessions: everything to the few, nothing to the many. The rulers earn, or at least pay for, their exalted position through suffering, and this suffering ennobles, if it does not exactly cleanse, the lies and betrayals upon which this position depends.
> (Greenblatt, 1985, p. 40)

Some critics argue that Henry in fact becomes more likeable as his limitations are revealed. His soliloquy is convincing evidence of the frail mortality he spoke about to his men for we see that he is as liable to self-pity as any other man. The ceremony his men consider to be his advantage can, he believes, because it compels 'poison'd flattery', induce delusions in a king of obedient loyalty in his subjects. Without it Henry has just discovered that his already wounded cause is even more vulnerable than he had thought. So, in his view, whatever the suspicions of his soldiers may be the 'wretch' and all 'private men' have 'the forehand and vantage of a king'.

The soliloquy is, in many ways, the climax of the concern with the problems of kingship throughout the tetralogy. This deep suspicion of the crown is not new to Henry. It 'fed upon the body' of his father and he tried it on accusing it as 'an enemy' (2 *Henry IV*, iv.v.158–77), but now, when he may be as close to death as his father was then, he feels some of Richard II's vulnerability about the hollow crown where the antic Death sits:

> Scoffing his state and grinning at his pomp;
> Allowing him a breath, a little scene,
> To monarchize, be fear'd and kill with looks;
>               (*Richard II*, iii.ii.163–5)

Henry's insistent interrogative assault indicates the hollowness of his power:

> What kind of god art thou, that suffer'st more
> Of mortal griefs than do thy worshippers?
> What are thy rents? What are thy comings-in?
> O Ceremony, show me but thy worth!
>               (iv.i.237–41)

The method of elaborate self-examination, as in a catechism, rattling the meaning out of commonly prized values, inevitably reminds us of Falstaff in his soliloquy on honour at the battle of Shrewsbury (*1 Henry IV*, v.i.127–40). Sir John is intent on setting aside the obligations of his class that would endanger his life and give him the 'grinning honour' Sir Walter Blunt achieves. Henry considers himself less fortunate than the average man because he cannot escape the burdensome, empty 'advantages' of kingship. The debate with his men teaches him that he must play the role of common man harder if he is to make them forget those advantages. In the St Crispin's Day speech we see him speak in unusually democratic terms which imply he feels a special closeness to his soldiers. Shakespeare forewarns us in this soliloquy that Henry's bitter, private view of his inferiors, typical of his class, is far different from the tactical stance he adopts on the morrow. Henry complains now that he is 'subject to the breath of every fool' and not fortunate enough to

> . . . sleep so soundly as the wretched slave
> Who, with a body fill'd and vacant mind,
> Gets him to rest, cramm'd with distressful bread;
> 
>                                    (iv.i.264–6)

He is envious that

> The slave, a member of the country's peace,
> Enjoys it; but in gross brain little wots
> What watch the king keeps to maintain the peace
> Whose hours the peasant best advantages.
> 
>                                    (iv.i.277–80)

These lines are often cut on stage, thus eliminating a bitter irony. A claim to maintain peace comes a little oddly from a king who has initiated a campaign of unprovoked aggression and is about to lead his men into a battle in which they seem likely to be slaughtered. Whatever he may think of the 'advantages' of his men he completely forgets or ignores the genuine pain and fear that they have expressed. With the huge, looming burden of his army's probable destruction on his conscience we are not surprised that, to avoid responsibility for it, he expresses a completely ungenerous sense of alienation from his men. His soldiers' mistrust of their leaders, on the evidence of the array of aristocratic duplicity Shakespeare dramatises throughout this tetralogy, is well founded, and yet they have asserted a willingness to fight lustily for him. Henry, however, does not celebrate their courage and loyalty, or sympathise with their fears – he concentrates instead on reviling them, minimising their travail, and feeling sorry for himself. Yet, even though he does not feel true fellowship, he will find a way to enact it.

There is a symmetrical structure to this scene, a descent into and out of solitude. The brief exchange with Erpingham, related to the one at the outset of the scene, reminds Henry of lords 'jealous of his absence', the collectivity of kinsmen and friends who share his task. It is this sense of himself as the shepherd of his flock which prompts his prayer to God (iv.i.285–301). It is the logical culmination of his soul-searching and, for the audience, the revelation of the deepest fears that must have troubled him since the outset of his career. Prince Hal seems to everyone, especially his father, to have little interest in government. In a subliminal way this may signal an attempt to escape the stigma of the 'crooked ways' that brought his father to the crown. In his 'transformation' he turns an apparent reluctance for kingship to his advantage. No matter how companionable he might seem he is, in fact, always apart. That is as clear in his first soliloquy (*1 Henry IV*, i.ii.188–210) and in his foreshadowing of Falstaff's banishment, 'I do, I will' (*1 Henry IV*, ii.iv.464), as it is in the soliloquy he has just completed. The combination of tenses he uses about Falstaff is poignant for it reveals that all of his relationships are subject to his kingly duties which, in the framework of his long-term planning, separate him from all men. He can talk to his men but, as we have just seen, he cannot be one with them. Called a fool by Williams he cannot respond as naturally as he might wish: 'I would be angry with you, if the time were convenient' (iv.i.202–3). But the time will never be convenient, not in his concealed identity in this scene, nor after the battle when, as king, he confronts Williams, because he cannot contend with one of his subjects as an equal no matter how many violets he smells.

If Henry deeply calculates his every move one suspects that it is

because he cannot afford to make a mistake. He does not talk
about the divinity that hedges a king, does not revel in his applica-
tion of power, ascribes all of his success to God and, in his prayer,
confronts the possibility of failure. He asks God to give his men
courage and to dispel their fears of the overwhelming numbers
facing them in battle (IV.i.285–8). He uncovers his deepest fear that
his army may be slaughtered on the morrow in payment for 'the
fault/My father made in compassing the crown!' (289–90). He lists
the extensive attempts at expiation he has undertaken (291–300).
In the sources it is clear that his prayer is intended to help release
his father's soul, as well as Richard's, from purgatory. But in
asking for pardon for blood Shakespeare implies that, despite all
his efforts to resist responsibility, he fears that he will himself be
held responsible 'for Richard's soul', a sin for which he begs a
postponed punishment now and eventual remission. It has been
played recently (SE, 1984) as a gabbled, terrified act of bribery,
very much in the spirit of his guilty father desperately promising crusades as atonement for usurpation and regicide. Michael
Pennington (ESC, 1986) played it in a similar manner, uttering
'More will I do' as an anguished guilt-wracked promise. It may not
have quite the numbness of Macbeth wearily registering the empti-
ness of a stolen crown but it does remind one of the torment of
Claudius who sees that to 'retain th' offence' makes prayer futile.
There is some ambiguity about the closing of Henry's prayer:

> . . . all that I can do is nothing worth,
> Since that my penitence comes after all,
> Imploring pardon.
>                    (IV.i.299–301)

for no interpretation of the second 'all' is entirely clear or persuasive. Gary Taylor resolves this problem by an emendation of
this second 'all' to 'ill', which clarifies it to provide precisely the
right balance

> between a pious Henry, aware like every true Christian of
> the inadequacy of his own or any man's penitence, and the
> audience's knowledge of the coming victory at Agincourt,
> which is a proof that God does not hold Henry responsible for

his father's sin and has accepted his efforts at atonement and his plea for pardon. Henry's closing confession of his own unworthiness is in fact the final proof to the audience that he is worthy. (Taylor, 1982, pp. 300–1)

This scene, the pivotal sequence in the play, builds to this moment when Henry, uncertain how God views him, is close to despair and in a situation close to that of a tragic hero. It is, however, a climactic moment often muffled in productions. Of the twenty promptbooks and scripts I have examined of major productions over the past sixty years, fifteen edit out significant parts of Henry's soliloquy, usually excising its closing four lines, eleven cut the part of the prayer relating to Richard, and some even the reference to the 'fault' of Henry's father. Branagh's film was a rare instance of presenting the prayer complete. Of the entire scene several productions cut somewhat more than a quarter of it (SE, 1943, 1971; SO, 1980; Olivier's film) while some cut from 15 to 25 per cent (SE, 1934, 1964; SO, 1956, 1966, 1989; ESC, 1986) and Branagh's film cut 35 per cent.

This scene is very much related to IV.i in *Richard II* and they are in many ways the two poles of the tetralogy. In his Gethsemane Richard, about to lose his crown, claims only to be king of his own griefs and forswears 'All pomp and majesty' even as he is prepared to lie like any other man 'in an earthy pit' (*Richard II*, IV.i.193–210). Gazing into a mirror which he claims beguiles him with flattery, he sees himself as a Christ betrayed by Judases and Pilates. Richard, remote from his people, relies too much on his unexamined assurance of power and never learns how to exercise it wisely. Henry IV, a transitional figure, wins the crown, some think, because he possesses the common touch (*Richard II*, I.iii.23–36), though he claims himself to practise a policy of remoteness (*1 Henry IV*, III.i.39–59), and this distance stirs up enemies against him. Henry V develops his own technique as a skilled variation on the practice of his predecessors. He reserves his self-pity for soliloquy rather than for the kind of public display which is Richard II's speciality. In his Gethsemane Richard loses his kingdom and his queen and is left alone trying unsuccessfully to come to terms with his mortality. Henry, in his crisis, aware of his isolation and mortality, nevertheless determines to assert a brotherhood with his subjects which brings him another kingdom and a queen. Richard concludes his Gethsemane by having to accept that he was dispensable, 'a true king's fall' (*Richard II*, IV.i.318), as he was 'conveyed' to prison. Henry, on the contrary, is aware that he is an indispensable figure of rising expectation which he can help to fulfil by his skilled performance as king. When he says 'The day, my friends, and all things stay for me' (IV.i.304) it appears that he has finally recognised that the responsibility he has so frequently sought to evade is an inescapable burden he must accept.

There are details in Holinshed about French arrogance prior to battle, dividing the spoils, playing at dice for the English, and devising a chariot in which to carry the captive Henry to Paris (Bullough, 1962, p. 394). Shakespeare uses some of this, along with details of the Constable's speech (IV.ii.15–37) in Hall, to develop his array of vainglorious French noblemen as a vivid contrast to the 'poor condemned English'. In IV.ii, as their overwhelming defeat draws closer, the French preen themselves in phrases of pitying disdain of the English: 'poor and starved band' (16), 'shales and husks of men' (18), 'island carrions' (39), 'beggar'd host' (43). The French believe they only have to blow on the English so that 'the vapour of our valour will o'erturn them' (24). They even think of clothing and feeding the English to make them respectable enough to be worth fighting (57–9). They view the battle as a show for their amusement (19–34) in which they can wreak revenge for the English triumph at Crécy, and are thereby shown to mire themselves as hip-deep in irony as they will shortly mire themselves in mud. They are presented in the play as a frieze of figures braying about war glory for, like the English lords, they are not markedly individualised. It is the unity of the English high-command that matters much more than any quirks of character, which is in distinct contrast to the idiosyncratic nature of several commoners. This battle campaign is not memorable for its generals or its battle actions. Afterwards it will not be easy to distinguish Westmoreland from Bedford, or Grandpré from Rambures, but we will have no problem remembering figures such as Pistol, Fluellen, Williams, Macmorris, the Boy, nor, along with these sharply etched figures, Henry himself.

There is a generosity and companionship in Henry's nobles when, in iv.iii, they address each other as 'noble', 'dear', 'good', 'kind', wish each other luck and commend each other's valour. Whereas the French, in iv.ii, mention God not once, the English, in iv.iii, refer to the deity nine times, six of the references being Henry's, and constantly ascribe any success they may have to God's will and aid. This habit, like Henry's insistence on mercy, the denial of pillage to his army, the protection of Church property, is in accordance with military treatises. Holinshed devotes a lot of space to describing Henry's skill in distributing his forces to make up for his inferiority in numbers, his use of stakes and ditches, and the positioning of his archers. Several pages of the chronicle are devoted to details of battle (Bullough, 1962, pp. 392–8), and include mention of Henry's own victory in combat over Alençon. Shakespeare's omission of such details may be part of the pattern of humility and total trust in God that military books prescribed for the Christian general (Jorgensen, 1956, pp. 88–98).

In Holinshed, Henry's battle-speech is essentially variations on his insistence that 'no man ascribe victorie to our owne strength and mighte, but onelie to God's assistance'. This emphasis on Henry's piety may have prompted Shakespeare to develop in Henry an anxiety about how God views his cause. The St Crispin's Day speech (iv.iii.18–67), however, is presented with a focus quite different from that of the chronicle. It arises directly from the episode Shakespeare invented of Henry's tour among his soldiers the previous evening. The speech is often given on stage in two phases, with Henry talking at the outset only to his generals (18–39) and only broadening his address to all of his soldiers in the latter half (SO, 1980, 1989; BBC TV). Since the Folio indicates that the army, 'host', appears at the outset of the scene, it is useful to have the king gather, as he did in his rallying cry at Harfleur, nobles and yeoman together, an emphasis Holinshed gives the speech: '. . . calling his captains and soldiers about him, he made to them a right grave oration'. In his film Olivier walks among his men and gathers a crowd from separate groups, visibly drawing them into unity. As his speech rises to its climax the camera pulls back to reveal an assembled mass charged with martial enthusiasm, 'an image of the leader as centre of his loyal army: from the psychological to the epic, from the monarch to the nation' (Holderness, 1985, p. 189). It has been presented as a man working extremely hard to encourage despondent men, only gradually gaining confidence in his oratorical powers (SO, 1966; ESC, 1986), in a conversational tone to a group of friends rather than a crowd (SE, 1964), or with a jocular attempt at intimacy (SO, 1989). Though Branagh, in his film, gives homage to Olivier by including a tracking shot of the king walking along a wagon, he emphasises the effect of the speech on several of the individual soldiers we have come to know. In this speech Shakespeare shows Henry treating his army as a single unit, a distinct advance on the alternating focus of the earlier battle-speech at the breach. That first speech is more off-the-peg, this one is tailored to a specific situation. There the emphasis was on fighting *for* Harry, here the emphasis is on fighting *with* him and for their own futures. Henry's bitter recriminations of the night, the panic of the lonely outsider whose father stole the crown, are firmly set aside. This situation demands unity and interdependence in which the king offers his all like his men. For Alan Howard Henry has now moved on to a spiritual equilibrium which he strives to transmit to his men. Each man is responsible for himself but will fare better if he responds to the interdependence of a common cause rather than the army's up-and-down line of command (Cook, 1983, p. 68). Henry now has some knowledge of the individual troops in his army gained since the rallying call at Harfleur where, urging his men to imitate the tiger, he had little to say of normal human behaviour. Here he speaks of his men returning to everyday human activities when they survive battle and we now have specific individuals to place in the rose-tinted future Henry prophesies. Productions often present a warmer intimacy in this speech, 'a little touch of Harry in the morning', by having Henry walk among his men, clap them on the shoulders, or playfully pull one man's cap over his eyes (SO, 1980), or have each soldier touch him as they move offstage to battle (SE, 1975). His first concern is to reassure his men that they have sufficient numbers for the task. In Holinshed Henry insists that it is good they are so few for, if they lose, the damage will be so much less for England. Shakespeare's king certainly does not use that argument. The possibility of death is only touched on lightly twice (20, 38). The emphasis is on togetherness and survival. Henry strings together a series of comforting words and images, which transports each soldier over the fearful battle directly ahead of him to picture him as a veteran basking in the peace of his English village long after this day. After battle each man 'comes safe home', each will 'live t'old age' and 'feast his neighbours' on St Crispin's Day. Each of these 'old men' will remember his noble companions 'Harry the king, Bedford, Exeter' in his home on that day because they are 'familiar in his mouth as household words' and to be celebrated in 'flowing cups'. In this cosy world each one will have enjoyed a long, fruitful, family life for 'This story shall the good man teach his son' on a memorial day that will never be forgotten 'From this day to the end of the world'. Henry assures men whom he knows do not expect to see the morrow, let alone old age, that in their long lives they will be immortalised as fortunate participants in one of England's most glorious victories. He mentions scars and wounds once, but only as emblems of glory to be shown after battle. Otherwise the horrors of war, so vividly evoked at Harfleur and by Williams on the previous evening, are entirely left out of Henry's account as he reinscribes these young men as sunny old codgers in a golden future, part of the legend of which we have heard the Chorus speak.

Productions of the play as an unblemished battle-hymn to the indomitable British present this speech as its most glorious verse and give no hint of the shrewd politics of its construction. As actors in the RSC 1975 production noted of Henry's offer to release men with no stomach for the fight (iv.ii.34–9): 'That's the oldest ruling-class ploy in the book', 'Where are you supposed to go if you do walk off, anyway? Slap into the enemy' (Beauman, 1976, p. 88). Henry is, in any case, safe in the offer given the nature of male bonding and the fear of losing face among one's fellows. It is that bonding, of course, to which he is appealing, as we can see in his emphasis in the speech on 'we' (seven times), 'our' (2), 'us' (2), 'brother/s' (2), 'fellowship'. However, to recoil from the speech as rhetorical cant is to miss the point Shakespeare is making. In soliloquy on the previous night Henry felt very far

from being part of a brotherhood. He knows, however, that he has
to forge his army into a brotherhood and levitate his men over
their fears expressed to him in the darkness if he is to have any
chance of success. He offers, therefore, what politically shrewd
soldiers in his situation generally have to offer, a powerful image
that compels conviction of a better future earned by bravery. We
recognise it as a performance and the question of whether he
believes it or not himself is less important than the fact that it is
exactly the right thing to say at this point for as one critic puts it,
'we respond to his success as we do when a political leader we
admire makes a great campaign speech: we love him for his
effectiveness' (Goldman, 1972, pp. 70–1). The speech is not
designed to work directly on us but to show us how it works on
his men and, perhaps, how it would probably have worked on us
had we been at Agincourt. Shakespeare's plays constantly show us
the labile nature of man and his ability to sustain contradictory
views. It has always been possible to whip men up to collective
enthusiasm and it will continue to be so whether we approve of it
or not. Gloomy night-time forebodings can give place to the
daylight optimism of hoping for the best, of looking past what
is staring you in the face. As Shakespeare shows us wars are
not actions of unalloyed bravery; there is a mixture of courage
and terror, of nobility and atrocity, an alternation which Henry
himself does not escape.

Henry goes beyond asserting identity with his men when he
says that this day's exploits will ennoble them and raise them to his
level: '. . . be he ne'er so vile,/This day shall gentle his condition'
(iv.iii.62–3). This promise of mingling blood ('he today that sheds
his blood with me/Shall be my brother' (61–2)) is very different
from the French attitude to blood represented by Mountjoy,
appalled that the blood of princes is soaked in mercenary blood
and that of vulgar peasant limbs (iv.vii.71–5). Henry suggests
nobility can be earned rather than inherited and brotherhood
achieved through a shared loss of blood rather than shared
bloodlines. Nothing, of course, will ever come of this offer which,
his men must know, in the urgency of the moment has only a
symbolic value. In less pressing circumstances the soldiers might
regard this as a lot of rot but, caught up in the terror of impending

battle they need to feel unity. We know what happens to a king who cannot inspire imaginations to such symbolic unity; he ends up dead like Richard at Pomfret Castle, or ravaged by guilt, like Henry IV, because the dubious legitimacy of his claim to the crown breeds schism in the realm. Henry shrewdly abandons the two-tiered appeal of his speech at Harfleur to suggest 'we're in it together', a theme he embroiders for the rest of the scene in the opportunity so handily provided for him by the French herald.

In Holinshed Henry assures his men that he will not accept ransom in his battle-speech. Shakespeare uses the St Crispin's Day speech to provide the groundwork of general democratic senti- ment to which Henry only later adds his specific determination to resist the privilege permitted him in the rules of warfare of his day. To the French herald he not only acknowledges the poverty of his army, he identifies himself with it: '. . . why should they mock poor fellows thus?' (IV.iii.92), 'A many of our bodies shall no doubt/Find native graves' (IV.iii.95–6). The emphasis on his own mortality is framed at the opening and closing of the speech (IV.iii.91, 122–5). Richard II had talked of wanting 'a little grave, an obscure grave' but only as a dramatisation of his loss of kingship. Henry suggests that he is willing to be buried in 'your dunghills' in order to secure his claim to France. Whether he actually means it we can never know because he is not called on to fulfil his promise. In clothing, as in attitude, he claims identity with his men in his emphasis on 'we', 'our', 'us' six times in as many lines:

> We are but warriors for the working day;
> Our gayness and our gilt are all besmirch'd
> With rainy marching in the painful field;
> There's not a piece of feather in our host –
> Good argument, I hope, we will not fly –
> And time hath worn us into slovenry.
>
> (IV.iii.109–14)

Henry expresses, in his speech to the herald, recognisable English values: plain, blunt John Bull outspokenness, disdain for showy ornamentation, a deceptive ordinariness which conceals hidden, sterling qualities, love of the underdog, and delight in the reversal of expectations whereby the plucky amateur beats the confident professional. If *Henry V* became a national anthem it is because its central figure so deliberately embodies qualities by which the English so often celebrate themselves. Henry, of course, cannot have wanted a sick, depleted army worn into slovenry, but he has the wit to exploit its crestfallen condition as a badge of honour. The chronicle sources mention the sorry nature of the army on several occasions. Shakespeare makes of such references a recurring refrain which accompanies Henry's assertions of identity with his men. If we add up all these references to the beleaguered army in France we see that, after a few brief references, it gradually becomes the focal point of several scenes: III.iii.54–6; III.vi.134–44, 148–50, 158–60, 163; III.vii.127–50; Chorus IV, 19, 22–8, 41–7; IV.i.85–91, 97–8, 112–22, 133–45; IV.ii.16–59; IV.iii.79–120. These passages make up 177 of the 1,259 lines after the campaign opens in France in Chorus III until Henry completely identifies with his army here in IV.iii – 14 per cent of the action, a much heavier emphasis than in any of the sources. Henry's refusal of ransom directly responds to the suspicions raised by Williams the previous night (IV.i.189–203). He rejected an earlier demand that he agree to ransom in a few brief lines (III.vi.148–50). Now he entwines his response in a long rejection of the insulting French presumption by presenting himself, in the most public way possible before his whole army, as determined to abandon privilege and fight to the death to demonstrate solidarity with his men. Henry enters battle with an army which seems to be united in pursuit of his campaign aims.

## · 4 ·

## 'Coupe la gorge':
## The battle of Agincourt

As battle opens we are immediately with one soldier whose aim in the campaign is quite different from that of Henry. The evocation of patriotic communion does not work on everyone. Pistol, the unreconstructed profiteer, has come to France 'to suck, to suck' like a horse-leech. Any belief that Henry turns base metal into gold by some alchemical process of inspirational rhetoric has to cope with the fact that the only detail of combat we actually see at Agincourt is Pistol's vaunting conquest of Le Fer. Glorious golden heroism there may be and we *hear* about some of it, but what we *see* is the persistence of base metal. As Hamlet noted, the majestical roof fretted with golden fire may dazzle us but cannot make us forget this quintessence of dust. The most surprising aspect of this play is the way Shakespeare presents the battle of Agincourt. Olivier's film version, which gives such an indelible picture of the battle, is liable to make us forget the battle Shakespeare structures. Soldiers preparing stakes, archers gathering in the woods, plumes and pennons, the great cavalry charge, the English dropping on the French cavalry from the trees, the air thick with arrows, all give us a comprehensive picture of battle activity. Branagh's film version, designed for devotees of mud-wrestling, is almost as comprehensive. Both versions, of course, completely cut IV.iv. Stage

versions usually make a good deal of the 'excursions' at the
opening of IV.iv to give us some image of the battle action
Shakespeare seems to have forgotten. We may get a stylised slow-
motion ballet of figures clashing swords (SO, 1956), the swirl of
banners, heavy drumming and arrows whistling through the air
(SO, 1980), or a tape of battle sounds, cavalry charge, flights of
arrows, clashing swords, groans and cries (SE, 1964, 1975). Terry
Hands said of his use of a sound-effects tape that it was necessary
in a period of naturalism and he was not courageous enough to
resist the audience's need of such aids to the imagination (Beauman, 1976, p. 195). The BBC TV production opened battle with
some sword-fighting. Adrian Noble had an army with pennons
and drums collecting behind York, a good deal of running back
and forth with swirling banners in excursions before settling the
action on Pistol and Le Fer (SE, 1984). These two figures, the
underbelly of the army, offer us an indelible parody of chivalry
and patriotic triumph. That explains, perhaps, why the scene was
omitted more often than not in productions prior to the 1920s.
One critic has objected to the idea that the scene is a parody, a joke
which so often in modern times reality plays on idealism (Frye,
1965, p. 29). Of course Pistol does not make us feel that Henry is
a foolish windbag but he reminds us that there are other agendas
being pursued at Agincourt besides the king's. The audience
usually believes Le Fer is wrong to be terrified of Pistol's fierce
gestures. In Bogdanov's ESC production Pistol entered with a
shopping cart, a scavenger looting the pockets of corpses. His
treatment of Le Fer was brutally violent, so much so that the Boy
was revolted by the savagery of his assault. The two clowns chew
up the language in trying to communicate with each other, and the
urgency to make profit or avoid death is so strong that, with the
Boy as translator, they succeed. Shakespeare seems to suggest that
if those actually at the battle can get things wrong, as Le Fer, like
Fluellen before him, mistakes Pistol's fake heroism as the real
thing, then we would do well to be wary of the trustworthiness of
all accounts of Agincourt such as those of the chronicles and of his
own Chorus.

   This battle lasts 219 lines from the first alarum – IV.iv (75), IV.v
(23), IV.vi (38) – up to IV.vii.83 when Mountjoy says 'the day is

yours', conceding victory to Henry. The farcical by-play between
Pistol and Le Fer provides 34 per cent of those lines. Some critics
see more logic in the quarto version which reverses IV.iv and IV.v.
I do not agree with this view but we have to confess that in either
order Shakespeare places emphasis on that aspect of battle, for
which the Chorus apologises (Chorus IV.48–53), lines which have,
in the last four RSC productions, been detached and inserted as a
preface to IV.iv. Yet, as I have noted, Shakespeare had plenty of
information about battle tactics, Henry's martial feats, and the
heroic deaths of York and Suffolk. Save for one brief reference he
ignores the first two and makes the last the substance of IV.vi.
'Brawl ridiculous' is not the only action representing Agincourt
but it is given considerable weight. It is evident that Shakespeare
may have been influenced in his presentation by his source play
*The Famous Victories of Henry the Fifth*. There are some similar
elements in it though with different emphases (Bullough, 1962,
pp. 333–7). There is a detailed description, not used by Shakespeare, of how Henry draws up his battle order (1,160–88). The
only indication of onstage combat is the stage direction *The
Battell* (after line 1,214). After the battle is over Henry briefly
laments York's death. Mention is made of the king's tents being on
fire (1,281–90), an oblique reference to the destruction of the
baggage train, but there is no mention of French prisoners killed
or boys slaughtered, important details in Shakespeare. In scene
xvii the clown Dericke attempts to force ransom from a French
soldier but the latter runs away while his back is turned. This is a
brief incident after the battle (1,291–313) and has little of the
pompous vaunting, verbal jests and puns through mistranslation
Shakespeare gives it in his extensive account. After all of the
French overconfidence, the demands for ransom, the dicing and
bets about who will take most prisoners, and Henry's unassuming
modesty and rallying cry, it can hardly be an accidental irony that
the first thing Shakespeare shows us is a Frenchman wailing for
mercy from a cocky, boastful Englishman we know to be one of
the least courageous in Henry's army. Le Fer is as far from the
vainglorious Dauphin as it is possible to imagine. Pistol is as far
from Henry as it is possible to be. Even though both impose
themselves on the French at Agincourt it is Pistol's performance

that we see and not Henry's. Pistol knows how to bluff and his
comic threats of cutting throats is only a much reduced version of
Henry's tactic of bluffing Harfleur into submission.

In hope of a nice profit from the ransom of his Frenchman Pistol
declares 'I will some mercy show' (iv.iv.63). Unfortunately for
Pistol the king is not of the same mind for, in less than a hundred
lines, Henry orders the killing of all prisoners. An opportunity for
blood-sucking is denied Pistol by Henry's blood-letting which is,
perhaps, why Shakespeare does not use this incident as a coda to
battle as in the source play. It reflects back to the issue of ransom
in Mountjoy's demands in iv.iii and forward to the killing of
prisoners in iv.vi. Clearly, later in the play (v.i) Pistol is not a man
who has profited from a windfall ransom. We have to assume that
Le Fer is one of those sacrificed on Henry's order. Some recent
productions have striven to bring home the reality of this slaughter
by enacting it on stage with Pistol cutting Le Fer's throat among
the prisoners killed on Henry's orders in iv.vi (SO, 1966, 1989),
thus adding a detail not in Shakespeare's text. In Bogdanov's
production, on the order to kill prisoners Pistol, with Le Fer in
his shopping cart, put his helmet over his prisoner's face hoping to
save him to gain ransom money. A rifle levelled at his head by an
officer forced him to slit Le Fer's throat and he angrily wheeled off
his now valueless hostage. There are over a dozen Frenchmen in
the play but only a few of them are developed in detail. Le Fer
appears in only one scene but is onstage as long and speaks as
many or more lines than Bourbon, Britaine, Rambures and
Grandpré. Shakespeare brings the slaughter home to us by letting
us get to know at least one of the captives. Maybe they were not all
as feeble and ineffective as Le Fer, but we can see that he is no
threat to the English and his sacrifice seems gratuitously futile. It
is a dismal contingency to lose your life because of submission to
a fraud as absurd as Pistol. Pistol's triumph comes fewer than a
hundred lines after Henry had looked forward to old veterans
showing scars and remembering glorious deeds 'with advantages' (iv.iii.50). We can imagine Pistol in the Eastcheap taverns
boasting of this success and embroidering his deeds at the bridge
'with advantages', a post-war parasitism prophesied by Gower
(iii.vi.66–79). Pistol will, as it turns out, have scars to turn to profit

in London from Fluellen's vigorously applied leek (v.i.78–83). A fragmentary detail in the source play becomes an extended sequence integrated by Shakespeare for a variety of ironical purposes. Shakespeare does not entirely demolish the heroism of war, for he also gives noble death a grave epitaph (iv.vi) as the 'mingled yarn' persists. Pistol's stumbling around with the French language as he tries to negotiate profit cannot entirely be forgotten when Henry woos Katharine. Henry's plain, blunt man approach is of a different order but it is, like Pistol's, certainly a performance. Henry's struggle with French reminds us that England's gain and Pistol's individual profit have something in common – the demand for submission to irresistible mastery.

It is at the end of the scene that the Boy, in his second soliloquy, informs us that another Eastcheap rogue, Nym, is, like Bardolph, executed for the 'advantages' he has parasitically sought. Juxtaposed to this account of corrupt experience is the innocent vulnerability of the Boy and the baggage train which, it turns out, is another less than glorious aspect of war Shakespeare emphasises, another detail the source play overlooked. A number of productions recently have supplemented Shakespeare's text by having the boys killed on stage. Having Frenchmen kill the boys at this point to protect Henry's reputation resolves an ambiguity that Shakespeare may have deliberately left in the text. The point at issue is whether the killing of the boys by the French happens before the killing of the French prisoners by Henry which makes his action a reprisal for a French atrocity. If, however, the boys are killed after the prisoners, Henry seems ruthless and the killing of the boys and the sacking of the royal tents could be a French reprisal. In 1975 Terry Hands had three faceless French deserters murder the boys here at the close of iv.iv and rearranged the text to ensure that Henry's action was seen as a reprisal, emphasised by having the French noblemen shocked and shamed when they discovered the slaughtered boys. This is a pattern followed in many variations in recent productions and is a problem to which I will return later.

The last times we saw the French noblemen (iii.vii, iv.ii) they were confidently chaffing each other about their coming triumph and scarcely able to contain their impatience to achieve it. Beneath all that glittering arrogance they can, however, behave like Le Fer, as we see in iv.v when they are yelling in panic and overwhelmed with shame. They do rally themselves and return to the battle, but the scene shows us, as briefly as possible, the swift reversal of expectation which is the most notable aspect of all accounts of Agincourt.

The next scene underlines the impression that the English are in command though the French have not yet yielded (iv.vi.1-2). We are given accounts of the companionship in sacrifice and the offstage deaths of York and Suffolk, the two most prominent English casualties (iv.vi.7–27). Shakespeare invents this farewell as a fugitive flourish of the waning values of the antique chivalric world in a war where the deeds of Pistol and the slaughter of boys and prisoners are prominent. It is a contrast Shakespeare had already exploited at Shrewsbury in placing Falstaff's pragmatic tactics of survival beside Hotspur's death. In contrast to the French concern with private honour York's dying words refer to service to his king.

Henry's peremptory order to his soldiers to kill their prisoners is a sharp, pragmatic decision set in contrast to this nobly heroic farewell. Many directors, troubled by this indication of ruthlessness in Henry's character as a blot on the escutcheon of an ideal king, have rearranged the text to clear up what they regard as inconsistencies in it. A common solution has been to cut iv.vi entirely (SE, 1943, 1946, 1964, 1971; SO, 1956) and to leave out all reference to the killing of French prisoners, as Olivier's and Branagh's films both do. The sacrifice of the noble epitaph to protect Henry's character eliminates some of the play's 'mingled yarn'. Often heavy cuts are made in iv.vi or the text rearranged, sometimes transferring iv.vi.36–8 to follow iv.vii.59, to ensure that Henry's execution of the French prisoners is clearly seen as a reprisal for the killing of the English boys at the baggage train (SE, 1951 cut 38.5 per cent; SE, 1975 86.8 per cent; SO, 1989 89.5 per cent). One solution is to run iv.vi and iv.vii together so that Fluellen enters as Henry leaves, indicating that they are in the same part of the battlefield, which gives the impression that Fluellen and Gower know Henry's action to be a reprisal. Another way is to have the boys stagger on stage retching blood to prompt Henry's

order (SO, 1966), or to cut the reference to killing prisoners in
IV.vi and to have Henry come onstage carrying a boy's corpse
before threatening to kill prisoners in IV.vii (SC, 1981). In a recent
production the Boy was killed on stage in a spectacular manner by
having him riddled with bullets, his shirt exploding with blood-
stained holes (SO, 1989). Of twenty productions in the last sixty
years that I have examined in detail only four adhere to the order
of events in Shakespeare's text (SE, 1934, 1937, 1984; BBC TV).
Directors often follow critics in justifying their rearrangement by
asserting that there is confusion in the source and in Shakespeare
about the order of events. Some critics have had no problem with
Henry's action: 'The impression which the incident was designed
to convey to . . . the original audiences, is not one of brutality, but
of a great commander's strength, decision and presence of mind at
the crisis of battle' (Wilson, 1947, p. xxxvii). Of early authorities
Gentili disapproved of Henry's action. Crompton, a lawyer, in
1599 excused it as 'a necessary occasion . . . by all reason allowed'
but considered it a misery of war and a disturbing action. This
indicates that Shakespeare's contemporaries could be critical of
Henry while recognising his practical problem of trying to control
the prisoners, who outnumbered his men, amid the threat of a
renewed French assault. As Bullough points out (1962, p. 364),
'Shakespeare does not shirk mention of an episode which might
seem to disprove Henry's humanity and mercy; more, he does not
defend it in the usual manner'. He points out that Fluellen's
disquisition on the matter in IV.vii indicates a deep ambivalence.
He also points out that there were many other versions of the
event available to Shakespeare much more favourable to Henry
and yet he chose the least favourable account of it. Yet, as I have
noted, critics and productions rearrange the text in their heads and
on the stage to ensure that Henry's action is unmistakably a
reprisal. Even recent productions which have tried to bring out the
ambiguities in the play have almost invariably balked at this
incident and fudged it. Terry Hands explains his rearrangement of
the text by expressing it as a sign of Henry's realism and determination: 'I think Henry is determined that war shall end. . . .
War must never again be a game – a game with prisoners ransomed
to fight another game' (Beauman, 1976, p. 200). He seems to

believe that by having the Boy killed on stage and rearranging the text he clarified Shakespeare's intention instead of replacing it with his own invention.

The research of modern historians has established that the plundering of the baggage train took place before battle and that, unconnected to it, Henry ruthlessly slaughtered his prisoners in the midst of battle, with a special squad of two hundred archers, when he feared a renewed French assault. In the chronicle sources Shakespeare used, Holinshed and Hall, it is presented as a pitiful and disgraceful action. In Holinshed's ordering of the phases of battle, which Shakespeare follows, there is no confusion. *Phase 1.* (a) The English archers inflict heavy losses; (b) the French flounder in confusion; (c) Henry in combat kills Alençon and two of his men; (d) many of the French throw away their armour, submit as prisoners and beg for their lives. Shakespeare translates this into the burlesque of Pistol's triumph over Le Fer, shows the French nobles in panic, and gives an account of the deaths of York and Suffolk, mentioned by Holinshed only in the list of the slain after the conclusion of battle. This reference to English losses sustains the idea in Shakespeare that, despite early success for Henry's forces, the French are still at work in a fight by no means yet settled. This helps to explain Henry's anxiety at the French counter-attack. *Phase 2.* (a) The English take many prisoners as battle continues; (b) in hope of easy spoil Frenchmen, hearing the English tents are unguarded, attack them, kill any servants that oppose them and make off with the booty; (c) Henry hears cries, without knowing them to be from defenceless servants, and mistakenly believes the French have gathered for another assault in which he fears the prisoners he has taken will join; (d) 'Contrarie to his accustomed gentleness', he orders that every man should

> incontinentlie slaie his prisoner. When this dolorous decree, and pitiful proclamation was pronounced, pitie it was to see how some Frenchmen were suddenlie sticked with daggers, some were brained with pollaxes, some slaine with malls, other had their throats cut, and some their bellies panched, so that in effect, having respect to the great number, few prisoners were saved. (Bullough, 1962, p. 397)

Hall's account, followed by Holinshed, called it a 'lamentable slaughter' and it is the most vividly detailed account of death at Agincourt. The account indicates that Henry kills the prisoners in anticipation of a renewed French assault and that it is not in any way connected with the slaughtering of the boys. The decision to kill the prisoners in Shakespeare is prompted by an alarum that is not related to action at the baggage train:

> [Alarum
> *Henry*: But hark! what new alarum is this same?
> The French have reinforc'd their scatter'd men.
> Then every soldier kill his prisoners;
> Give the word through.
>
> (iv.vi.35–8)

Because Henry asks the question it is evident that he does not know the source of the alarum. His order is, as in Holinshed, a precautionary measure to give himself better odds in face of a renewed attack. Gary Taylor outlines similar ideas to the ones suggested here. He is so convinced of Henry's cold-bloodedness that he takes the unusual step of including a stage direction in his Oxford text, '[*The soldiers kill their prisoners*]', after Henry issues his order (iv.vi.36) and Noble staged it in this fashion in his production (SE, 1984). The argument to justify this is that the prisoners brought on in this scene are only there for the precise purpose of having their throats cut to indicate what Taylor (1982, p. 32) calls Henry's 'personal and decisive contribution to battle'. It could be argued that this violence on stage, rather like the garrotting of Bardolph in Noble's production, distorts Shakespeare's intention by modifying the text to indict Henry just as much as the cuts or rearrangements of the text in the past exempted him from any blame. Shakespeare often modified the details of history to suit his own purposes and could have done so here to clear Henry of the charge of unprovoked ruthlessness, as productions so often do on his behalf. In fact, however, he does the opposite and closes a loophole in the chronicles that might be used to excuse Henry. Henry's action has been termed a 'prudential' strategy, yet another example of planning ahead to maximise his advantage.

There is a third phase of the battle in Holinshed, which Shakespeare follows, to which I will return later. First, however, it is necessary to look at one of the strangest episodes in the play (IV.vii.1–51). On stage Gower and Fluellen are usually placed at the site of the baggage train with the dead body of the Boy, along with other corpses, as vivid evidence of the French atrocity (SE, 1975, 1984; SO, 1956, 1966, 1980; ESC, 1986). Bogdanov brought on a wagon piled high with corpses under a tarpaulin, among which the Boy's body was prominent, and his glazed eyes were closed in tearful fury by Fluellen. There is no evidence in the text that the scene should be played in this manner, something which is easily accomplished in a black-out on the modern stage but by no means as easily on Shakespeare's stage. Fluellen and Gower could have carried dead boys on with them but one would expect such a striking effect to have left some evidence in the text. Holinshed makes it clear that the tents and pavilions where the slaughter occurred 'were a good waie distant from the army'. Henry is still clearly expecting further attacks from the French. It makes no sense at all that Fluellen, Gower, and later in the scene Henry and his generals, have retreated from confrontation with the French to the baggage train which was vulnerable exactly because it was so far from the protection of the English army. Both Olivier's and Branagh's films recognise this and adjust their scripts accordingly. Some of Shakespeare's lines are used as supplementary splices in their elaborate visual effects. Of the 219 lines of battle Olivier and Branagh both use only 31. All references to the killing of French prisoners are cut and both films present Henry as retiring from the front lines to discover the slaughter of the boys at the baggage train only when the fighting is concluded. Branagh, of course, makes the climax of his sequence the spectacular, extended three-and-a-half-minute tracking shot of Henry carrying a boy's corpse right across the devastation of the battlefield. The hallowed tradition of staging this scene at the baggage train misses Shakespeare's intention. News has also arrived of the killing of the French prisoners which, Gower asserts, is Henry's reprisal. Though Gower and Fluellen have time to chat we must assume that they are still at a critical front of the battle because Gower asserts the killing of the boys was done by French cowards who 'ran from battle':

'Tis certain there's not a boy left alive; and the cowardly rascals that ran from the battle ha' done this slaughter; besides they have burned and carried away all that was in the king's tent; wherefore the king most worthily hath caus'd every soldier to cut his prisoner's throat. O, 'tis a gallant King!

(IV.vii.5–10)

The sequence makes much more sense as an exchange during a lull in the fighting near the front lines. A report has arrived of the killing of the boys, an event which must have happened after IV.iv and probably after IV.vi since news of it has not reached Henry in that scene. News has also arrived of the killing of the French prisoners. Shakespeare not only follows the order of events in his source – he makes it even clearer that the two events are quite independent. Gower has received two pieces of information and automatically relates them so that the English action is praise-worthy and the French one damnable. In his view the gallant Henry has paid back the barbarous French. Gower is not con-sciously distorting events but through him Shakespeare shows us how, by reflex, patriotism adjusts events to create the heroic. Critics and directors, however, assume that Gower's confusion, which sanitises Henry's reputation by reversing the order of events we see, is Shakespeare's and adjust the text to make Gower right. They do this in a play where confusion, bluff and contra-diction are seen to be an inevitable part of battle and where the heroic account of the Chorus is subject to repeated correction.

Fluellen is a strange character who often wins, in his eccentric comedy, the admiration of critics, especially because he smokes out Pistol and punishes his pretensions. The Welshman is often played on stage as the quicksilver, spry terrier that Esmond Knight makes of him in Olivier's film. Some of the excesses of his language are pruned and in most productions his strange contribu-tion to IV.vii is usually cut. The lines can be used, if given in full, to reveal a not very bright, obsessive, self-important windbag. Tim Wylton (BBC TV) and William Dunlop (SO, 1989) played the role successfully, though in different ways, as a slow-witted, grumpy figure braver than Pistol but certainly no brighter and scarcely less pompous. The killing of the boys is an atrocity appalling enough in and of itself. Fluellen reacts to it typically in terms of his obsession believing the massacre to be especially bad because it violates his beloved 'disciplines of war'. This is merely the extremest example of his fantastically skewed sense of proportion.

Fluellen's digression into a comparison of Alexander the Great and Henry is one of the oddest moments in the play, evidence of his babbling complacency, effectively emphasised in the BBC TV production by having him noisily eat an apple throughout his lecture. But even with someone so self-important it is difficult to bring off this sequence on a corpse-strewn stage, which is, perhaps, why it is so often cut. When it is not situated at the baggage train, as indeed it should not be, we can concentrate on the way the thick-skinned Fluellen uses the report of the tragedy to unload, with stunning irrelevance, some of his military lore in comparing Henry to Alexander to justify the killing of prisoners. He follows the rules of the familiar rhetorical exercise of *comparatio*, which moves from origins and birthplace on to similar biographical events in the lives being compared. Classical parallels weigh so heavily in Fluellen's inflexible mind that he can only issue praise if a modern action or person can be related to a prototype of the ancients. A slow-witted man, caught in an endless elaboration of phrases, he is a very concrete thinker who believes his comparison is apt because Alexander and Henry were both born beside rivers and 'there is salmons in both'. It is in his completely inappropriate comparison of Henry's killing of the French prisoners with Alexander's killing of Cleitus when drunk that we understand Shakespeare's intention in this sequence. Alexander killed his close friend when he was 'in his rages, and his furies, and his wraths, and his moods, and his displeasures and his indignations' (IV.vi.30), or, to put it in a nutshell, when he was completely out of control. Gower interrupts, knowing that Fluellen is off the mark: 'Our king is not like him in that: he never kill'd any of his friends' (IV.vii.38–9). His failure to fasten on the main flaw in the parallel prompts the audience to recognise it. Alexander 'in his ales and in his angers' killed one friend. Henry, in stone cold sobriety, killed thousands of enemies in a ruthlessly determined act to ensure victory. We are reminded at this point how coldblooded Henry can be as Fluellen, to salvage his comparison, recalls the rejection of Falstaff when the king 'turned away the fat knight with the great belly doublet' (IV.vii.45). Fluellen is aware that his parallel is not exact for Henry did not directly kill Falstaff as Alexander killed Cleitus, though we recall the Hostess's assertion that he 'kill'd his heart' (II.i.85–6). He also knows that when Henry turned away Falstaff he was very clearly 'in his right wits and his good judgement' (IV.vii.44). We also know of how other 'friends', Scroop, Bardolph and Nym, have become subjects of Henry's 'good judgement' in this play. This is the only mention of Falstaff in the play after the report of his death (II.iii) and we cannot take the placing of this reminder, which has a poignancy of which Fluellen is completely unaware, to be accidental. Of all the strategies in Henry's career the rejection of Falstaff and the killing of the prisoners are the two most ruthless examples, which is why Shakespeare connects them and contrasts them with Alexander's rash but uncalculated act. Fluellen also fails to register the fact that Alexander, the Pig of Macedon, was considered by many to be a symbol of the unappeasable lust for blood and territory. Henry, who constantly asserts that such a motive is irrelevant to his own conquest, would hardly relish the comparison with Alexander. Henry has killed one set of prisoners and is quite prepared to kill some more, as we learn in his response to the third phase of battle, to which I can now return, and which has developed while Fluellen has been eulogising his king.

*Phase 3.* (a) In Holinshed the English draw up their battle order again and in a 'fresh onset' assault the French forces; (b) since they are again successful we must assume that further prisoners are taken. Holinshed concludes this phase of battle with Henry's threat to kill yet more prisoners:

> Some write, that the king perceiving his enemies in one part to assemble togither, as though they meant to give a new battell for the preservation of the prisoners, sent to them an herald, commanding them either to depart out of his sight, or else to come forward at once, and give batell: promising therewith, that if they did offer to fight againe, not onelie those prisoners which his people alreadie had taken; but also so many of them as in the new conflict, which they thus attempted should fall into his hands, should die the death without redemption. (Bullough, 1962, pp. 397–8)

Shakespeare records precisely this information as part of his own
account, showing the king's anger when he comes on stage
(iv.vii.52), which indicates either that he is only now reacting to
the slaughter of the boys or that he is angry that the French persist
in threatening to fight. The prisoners Henry brings on with him in
this scene are not the same ones he brought on in iv.vi. Fluellen
and Gower have indicated that those prisoners have been slaughtered. We have to assume that this is another batch of prisoners
captured during the exchange they have just had, one of the
explanations for Shakespeare's elaboration of the comparison of
Henry with Alexander. The mistake critics and directors make is
in assuming that the action of iv.vi and iv.vii all refer to one event
when, in fact, we are clearly dealing with different phases of battle.
The French still on 'yond hill' seem poised for attack and Henry,
to compel submission, threatens to equalise the numbers in the
two armies by killing more prisoners, the ones he has gained since
the slaughter of the first batch and any more he may take. Shakespeare had Holinshed's warrant that the threat effected instant
capitulation: 'The Frenchmen fearing the sentence of so terrible a
decree, without further delaie parted out of the field' (Bullough,
1962, p. 398). I have gone into this in considerable detail because
the sequence has scarcely ever been understood and has almost
certainly never been correctly presented on stage to reflect Shakespeare's intention. That can be done quite simply by presenting the
text without interference in the order in which Shakespeare wrote
it – a novel idea, granted, but worth a try.

The threat to prisoners on stage is very real in those recent
productions in which the slaughter ordered in iv.vi is conducted
on stage (SO, 1966, 1989; SE, 1984; ESC, 1986). Throat-cutting, as
a cocomitant of war, is carefully prepared for in the text, as one
critic has noted (Merrix, 1972, p. 332), by a dozen references from
a variety of characters: ii.i.23–5, 67–8, 69; iii.ii.105, 126; iii.vi.42–
6; iv.i.191, 224; iv.iv.14–15, 32–3, 35–6, 37. Henry is constantly in
doubt about whether he can contain his prisoners and so
slaughters them and threatens to continue doing so to avoid any
possible reversal of his improbable success. His continuing uncertainty expressed to the French herald (iv.vii.80–3) is a para-
phrase of Holinshed, but in the chronicle the lines are a sarcastic

pretence because the herald only comes on the following day after
Henry has celebrated victory. Shakespeare telescopes all these
events so that amid the counter-attacks and the king's desperate responses to them Henry's doubts are only resolved when
Mountjoy says 'The day is yours' (83). This statement closes one
of Shakespeare's strangest battles for, as Terry Hands says, it is
a battle

> begun by three clowns, fought over boys, luggage and prison-
> ers, and ended in confusion. Where, other than the minds of
> journalists and academics, is the famed, tub-thumping, war-
> mongering patriotism? (Beauman, 1976, p. 204)

In Hands's production Henry burst into tears at news of his
victory and collapsed on the ground in relief from the almost
unbearable tension.

The manner of this victory, as the crowning glory of Henry's
reign, bears the stamp of his style. The reversal of expectations
is Henry's speciality, caught at the outset of the play (I.i) in
the language of extreme contrasts in him: 'wildness mortified'
(26), 'angel . . . offending Adam' (28–9), 'The strawberry . . . the
nettle' (60), 'wholesome berries . . . fruit of baser quality' (61–2).
Throughout his career Henry provokes stunned responses by this
manipulation of extreme contrasts: *1 Henry IV*, I.ii.188–210,
III.ii.160–1, IV.i.97–110, v.i.52–69, v.iii.48–50; *2 Henry IV*,
IV.iv.67–78, IV.v.178–80, v.ii, v.iv. Anyone who underestimates
Henry pays for it – Hotspur, Falstaff, the Dauphin, Canterbury,
Scroop, Bardolph, the French generals. Shakespeare understands
and seeks to show the method by which Henry became so famous.
The battle, like his career, acquires the quality of miracle because
it goes so much against the odds.

It is typical of Fluellen to choose such an inappropriate moment
to go on with his nationalistic strutting, rejoicing in the reflected
glow of Henry as a Welsh hero. Henry realises at once that in the
'hot as gunpowder' Fluellen he has the perfect instrument to hand
for a jest which will allow him to display the common touch even
as he reasserts his awesome status as king. From a practical
viewpoint this is the only available material with which to occupy
the stage between the French submission and the announcement

of battle losses. The revelation by Henry of the trick he has played
on Williams is usually done lightheartedly on stage to remind us
quite clearly of the prankster Hal we knew in the earlier plays.
This manipulation of roles, Henry appearing alternately as commoner and king, inevitably reminds us of the way he ragged
Francis and Falstaff in the Boar's Head. The reason why we are
always thinking of the two bodies of the king in relation to Henry
is that he so frequently emphasises his mere mortal body by
acting as thief, customer, drawer, bread-chipping pantler, common soldier: a variety of non-regal roles, which cumulatively
convey his pretence of everyman. Eschewing, during this campaign, a stance of awesome majesty among his men he also
presents himself to God as a humble suppliant who makes no
special claims for himself.

The events in this play appear to relate to the rites of passage
described by Arnold van Gennep and of liminality embroidered
in the works of Victor Turner. The levelling of distinctions in
Henry's loss of identity in his tour among his soldiers seems to
place him in a liminal phase displaying values Turner terms
'communitas'. The Chorus implies that Henry, in a sacramental
communion, is sealed into a bond of fellowship with his army,
or what van Gennep terms transition rites leading to rites of
incorporation. In iv.i, however, the audience observes Henry drift
into separation rather than into a liminal phase of levelling, as his
soliloquy and prayer clearly underline. The rite of incorporation
is presented in his battle-speech to his 'band of brothers' in a
celebration of the values of 'communitas'. Rather than declining to
the soldiers' level Henry claims to 'gentle' their condition and
raise them to his, and he emphasises their equality in his refusal of
ransom. This marriage to his people will be augmented by his
marriage to Katharine.

The glove filled with crowns that is given to Williams is a king's
largess which firmly indicates to the soldier his place as a subject
and re-establishes the hierarchy that Henry momentarily abro-
gated when it was necessary to bind his men into unity in his
assertion of brotherhood. We might wonder, of course, why
Henry rewards this conspicuous member of the awkward squad.
When he calls Williams 'fellow' (iv.vii.57) he is very far from

meaning 'brother'. Whatever part Williams took among the 'band
of brothers' in the battle, it does not 'gentle his condition'. The
good, plain, blunt Williams is rewarded for his sterling courage as
a representative of an army which may have doubted Henry but
which determined 'to fight lustily for him' in any case. It is the
turn next of the good, plain, workaday warrior-king to receive his
reward, which turns out to be, in the announcement of battle
casualties, a miracle. That the rites of incorporation bonding
Henry to his men was a stratagem of temporary convenience is
made clear by the careful differentiation among the battle casualties, 'prisoners of good sort' (iv.viii.73), 'besides common men'
(77), 'gallant gentlemen' (82), 'gentlemen of blood and quality',
'None else of name, and of all other men/But five and twenty'
(103–4). We can see that if Williams and the other commoners we
have come to know had been killed at Agincourt they would be
merely a number and not a name among the English dead. On
stage we usually observe Henry's amazed relief at the stunning
disparity in battle losses. Christopher Plummer spoke in hushed
humility (SO, 1956). Jack Wetherall burst into tears and had to be
comforted (SO, 1980), and Alan Howard, believing that this
moment was like a sudden discovery of God, emphasised the line
'O God, thy arm *was* here!' (iv.viii.104) to reveal it. The way of
phrasing the line reflects back to Henry's prayer, his hope for aid,
his deep uncertainty about whether he would get it, which is now
resolved for him as he interprets it as God's signal that the wages
of his father's sin are not to be exacted from him. Although given
the opportunity to take away his crown God has allowed him to
lead his men into the very jaws of death and escape almost
unscathed, proving that his risky gamble has paid off.

In actual history the French lost around 7,000 men and the
English at most 500. Agincourt did not, of course, win France for
Henry, though Shakespeare's extreme telescoping of events
implies that it did. It gave him a chance to recover from what
had promised to be a disastrous campaign, for the victory was
followed by twenty months of diplomacy. It also supplied him
with the financial and patriotic support to carry out the much
more significant Normandy campaign of 1417–19 which led to the
Treaty of Troyes in the spring of 1420, some four-and-a-half years

after the victory at Agincourt. By eliminating those years Shakespeare makes the triumph seem even more miraculous than it was.
Henry himself affects to believe that God's aid alone can explain
the miracle:

> When without stratagem,
> But in plain shock and even play of battle,
> Was ever known so great and little loss
> On one part and on th' other? Take it God,
> For it is none but thine.
>
> (IV.viii.106–10)

Whereas the French speak of God or swear by him only ten times
in the play, the English make eighty such references. Henry, who
makes thirty-eight of them, is constantly evoking divine aid.
Henry's victory is not, however, as Shakespeare evidently knew
and must have believed Henry himself knew, entirely 'without
stratagem' and due solely to God's aid. We have to suspect from
the way Shakespeare organises his material and scarcely mentions
Henry's troop deployment, outlined in such detail in the chronicle
sources as key contributing elements in the victory, that Shakespeare means us to speculate about a likely explanation for this
amazing disparity in casualties. Shakespeare means us to ask,
though scarcely anyone ever does so, how many of the ten
thousand dead were prisoners slaughtered by Henry's cold-
blooded strategy, a strategy about which he is more deliberately
clear than any of his sources. In subsequent history Henry was
thought to be one of God's favoured warriors, and in the past
productions have always, with only a few recent exceptions, so
featured him. Shakespeare allows us to see how fervent Henry is in
shaping that reputation himself on the one hand, while letting us
see, on the other hand, a very practical explanation of the miracle
wherein God would seem to help those who help themselves.

## · 5 ·

# 'She is our capital demand': The Treaty of Troyes

The purpose of v.i is to resolve the episodic relationship between Pistol and Fluellen and to establish firmly the mood of comedy with which the play concludes. Pistol's pretence of bravery is finally challenged and punished. He is placed in the structure of the play in relation to the Chorus. The Chorus idealises Henry in an account that is a kind of nationalist bragging while Pistol, a ridiculous braggart, provides a burlesque of heroism. After he has been made to grovel and eat the leek it is clear that Pistol can be seen by everyone for what he is, which is more than can ever be said of Henry, who is the most accomplished role-player of whom Shakespeare ever wrote, if only because, unlike the villains, Iago, Edmund, Iachimo and others, he is never found out. Henry is just as effective in getting his performance accepted when we last see him as he was when we first saw him. Fluellen threatens Pistol with 'more sauce to your leek' (v.i.45). The French do not have to eat a leek at Troyes but they do have to swallow something less palatable, all of Henry's terms. He offers a certain amount of sauce to go with them.

In a play which has been concerned with war from its opening lines we finally emerge into the quieter, civilian world of peace. The dominant figure in v.ii, however, is a man who claims to be a soldier first and foremost. He is, to borrow Othello's phrase, 'unused to the melting mood'. From Barnabe Rich's *Farewell to Militarie Profession* Shakespeare could have seen how an abrupt, clumsy lover could elicit sympathy rather than disdain from Elizabethans and could appeal to women. The role of plain, blunt man, something of an unbroken colt unpractised in courtierly ways, has worked for him as heir apparent, as king and warrior. He has every reason to believe it is worth giving the role another airing when he becomes a suitor for marriage. His bluff heartiness does not hide the iron grip he has on France in a velvet glove, but it does pretend to make it seem like a benign conquest. Some recent productions have striven to indicate that the sprightly woo-ing sequence is a thin veneer which cannot appease a bitterly vanquished nation, a scarcely tolerable tissue of hypocrisy organ-ised by public relations men with the French king almost choking on the English terms (SO, 1966), a charade in which the com-placent English ignore the boiling resentment of the French (SO, 1989), placarded as 'The Deal' attended by blood-splotched masked figures representing the French dead of Agincourt (SC, 1969). Shakespeare ensures that we do not forget the damage Henry's campaign has done to France by allowing Burgundy to give a lengthy account of it (v.ii.23–67), though it is often, unfortunately, radically cut in production. This speech draws together all of the agricultural images spread across this tetralogy to give an elegaic picture of neglect and disorder. What has been lost sight of in Richard II's 'farming' of the land to bankruptcy, in the civil wars that ploughed up England in Henry IV's reign, and in Henry V's adventure in France, is that civil order of good, balanced government so frequently compared to the skills of good husbandry. Wars of conquest may exercise the professional skills of soldiers but they make everyone else into victims. Burgundy describes how the wild, uncultivated fields produce their harvest of wild children – savages, not good citizens (54–64). This speech is the culmination of a whole sequence of references in the play to war's victims: III.iii.1–43; Chorus IV.22–8; IV.i.136–41; IV.ii.16–23, 39–55; IV.iv; IV.vi.37–8. If we total up all lines devoted to the ravages of war and its victims climaxed in Burgundy's powerful speech we find close to 220 lines (6.8 per cent of the play), which gives us a constant sense of a world needing restoration to prosperous fertility. In his characteristic fashion Henry places the responsibility for such a renewal on to the French themselves (v.ii.68–73) which they can only bring about by acceding to his terms.

The wooing scene has no basis in history and it is developed out of a much briefer and infinitely simpler scene in *The Famous Victories* (Bullough, 1962, pp. 338–40) where there is something like the blunt reality of a peasant courting his lass, somewhat reminiscent of Breughel, upon which Shakespeare's Henry works such elaborate variations. In the abridged source play the wooing sequence occupies fifty lines (1,360–409); the substance of the sparring between the lovers lasts only thirty-five lines (1,370–404). There is no impediment caused by problems with language for neither French, broken French, nor broken English are used. There is also some implication of political purpose in Katheren's role, for Henry believes she has been sent by her father when she asks him to drop some of his unreasonable demands. Shakespeare's wooing sequence, at nearly one hundred and eighty lines (v.ii.99–277), is five times as long. In the source Katheren speaks almost as many lines as Henry, far from the case in Shakespeare. Shakespeare's expansion is devoted almost entirely to Henry's repeated protestations of his inadequacy as a courtier, which occupy 96 lines (v.ii.121–30, 132–67, 177–86, 194–208, 219–43) compared to the mere six lines in the source play (1,373–8), in which Henry expresses his inability to act like those who 'spend half their time in woing'. Save for the Hostess in a couple of early scenes and the French lesson (III.iv) we see no women in the brutally masculine world of war. Until v.ii we see women on stage for only 6.4 per cent of the lines. The turn away from obsessive masculine compulsions is signalled by placing three women in the last scene, though Queen Isabel's role is often cut (SE, 1975, 1984; SO, 1989), and centring the action on a man in pursuit of a woman. To beguile Katharine Henry affects the ordinary humanity that had so beguiled his soldiers in his St Crispin's Day speech. The skill deployed here is that of apparent improvisation, but as Castiglione and others in the Renaissance well understood, the impromptu character of an improvisation is often itself a calculated mask, the product of careful calculation. (Greenblatt, 1980, p. 227)

It is possible, of course, for those who want, to take this sequence at face value as a conventional happy ending, but there are clues for those who wish to find it disturbingly ambiguous. It may be that Henry, mistaken for an irrepressible clown by the Dauphin, wants to show how he can take that role and make France pay for it. Or it may be an elaborate charade to save the French sense of dignity by pretending to give Katharine a prerogative of choice where none exists. On the surface this scene is the final exploration of a theme, prominent in the tetralogy, and especially emphasised in this play, the inability of people to comprehend each other. The scene works best, I believe, when, despite linguistic problems, we are made aware that, beneath the charm of their sparring, they both know it is a game they are playing and that Henry is matching himself to a woman who knows such games must be well played. Henry urges Kate to disregard his lack of courtierly skills and physical attributes and accept the loyalty of his good heart because it will endure long after the attractions of youth have declined into age. This long-term view of how he will improve over time is consistent with everything we know of Henry: '. . . the elder I wax, the better I shall appear' (230). It is a description, as it happens, of the successful technique he has used in wooing England, that contrast between his unpromising youth and the wise maturity on which Canterbury commented at the outset (1.i.23–59). His role-playing does not abash Katharine, who is sprightly enough to challenge him wittily about how it is possible for her to love the enemy of France (168–9). Both Alan Howard and Ludmila Mikael (SE, 1975) believed, when performing the wooing, that this question indicated that Henry had met his match and changed the direction of the scene to make a merely political match become something more (Beauman, 1976, p. 225). We cannot forget, however, the political grip and the hunger for land behind the wooing, as Henry reminds us: 'I love France so well that I will not part with a village of it, I will have it all mine' (172–3). All Katharine, his capital demand, can do to maintain her dignity is to resist stubbornly and make him play the suppliant lover much longer than he had expected, as we gather from his growing impatience. He may start out by asking 'Canst thou love me?' (192), but her resistance forces him in the end to ask 'will you have me?' (225), and to acknowledge that he needs her to be a 'good soldier-breeder' (200). The scene is often cut quite radically so that Henry's seemingly artless manoeuvring and his impatience do not get a chance to develop fully. Branagh's film cuts nearly half of it. Only five of the twenty modern productions I have looked at in detail cut less than a quarter of the scene (SE, 1937, 1964; SO, 1956, 1966; BBC TV). Henry laid successful siege to Harfleur, and when he seemed helplessly vulnerable at Agincourt he achieved a swift victory. When he lays siege to the helplessly vulnerable Katharine she resists his peremptory 'clap hands and a bargain' approach and refuses to capitulate. She exercises the only prerogative left to her, which is to make him work hard to achieve her. Shakespeare devotes 261 lines to the winning of Harfleur, 219 lines to the battle of Agincourt and 297 lines (v.ii.68–365) to the winning of Katharine.

The scene contains substantial contradictions for an actor to negotiate. This self-proclaimed 'plain soldier' does manage to use complex rhetorical figures, though he claims ignorance of such artifice, to tell Kate that she is an angel, that he loves her cruelly, that her 'voice is music', that she is a divine goddess. Despite her protestations of modesty he wins a kiss from lips he asserts contain witchcraft. He may not be an inventive lover but he is a remarkably talkative one. There is often a paradox for an audience watching a handsome and graceful actor describing himself as a roughneck. No one ever doubts that Olivier, whatever assertions about crudeness he may make, is anything other than a suave, dashing hero. It has been argued that the warrior returning to peace from rugged success in battle is related to the resolution of the classic Western (Davies, 1988, p. 37). Olivier, however, scarcely comes close to Gary Cooper or James Stewart as 'aw-shucks' lovers, clod-hopping around feminine grace. Some actors, such as Richard Burton, Alan Howard and Kenneth Branagh,

have managed to infuse greater conviction into the role of diamond-
in-the-rough. Douglas Rain (SO, 1966) gave a very broad interpretation of a clumsy farmer careering about in a lady's parlour.
Pennington (ESC, 1986) went through the wooing as a boring
chore, speaking his compliments mechanically as patronising in-
dulgence to a sulky, resistant and scarcely ever smiling Katharine,
the coldness of political calculation very much to the fore.

On the return of the French court Henry engages in an
elaborate exchange with Burgundy (v.ii.278–314) full of sly sexual innuendoes and puns, very much in the vein, as one critic
observes, of a Middleton London marriage comedy (Gilbert,
1953, p. 60). The coarse, masculine jesting relates back to
Burgundy's earlier speech about the need to cultivate the devastated garden of France (v.ii.24–67). A promised fertility is
suggested in vigorous sexual puns around 'conjure', 'spirit',
'circle', 'wink and yield', 'handling'. When Henry asserts he cannot see the French cities he seeks because the maid blinds him to
them Charles VI suggests they become, by some transformation
of the girdled walls, the maid herself. Henry, who has breached the
cities, will do the same to Katharine to bring fertility to the land he
has devastated. Henry has asked Kate to compound with him a
boy 'half French, half English, that shall go to Constantinople and
take the Turk by the beard' (206–7). The audience perceives a deep
irony in this desire for another aggressive male, for it knows that
the boy, Henry VI, was so lacking in martial skills that he lost all
the territory his father is here winning. In the twenty modern productions I have discussed, most, and usually all, of the shrewdly
placed exchange with Burgundy was cut. When productions miss
out this final transit from rough soldier to skilled politician they
eliminate the play's final example of the enigma with which Shakespeare confronts the audience throughout – who exactly is Henry?

This tetralogy began with the double divorce of Richard II
''twixt my crown and me,/And then betwixt me and my married
wife' (*Richard II*, v.i.72–3). After his loss of his land and his
French wife civil war ravaged England. Henry V in his foreign
campaign seems to bring unity to his land and a promise of unity
with France as he moves out of the isolation of bachelordom into
marriage with his French wife.

# Epilogue: 'This star of England'

Just as Henry has apologised for his clumsiness, so we are given one final apology by the Chorus for Shakespeare's 'rough and all-unable pen'. By this time we know that in this account of 'mighty men' the real skill is to be found precisely in the technique of 'Mangling by starts the full course of their glory' for which the Chorus apologises. Shakespeare extracts one last triumph for the complex realism of his method. When he achieves his miraculous victory Henry believes that the pardon he implored for his father's sin has been granted. The Epilogue reminds us that those who took over his realm 'lost France and made his England bleed' (12). We are made aware that there are longer-term consequences to Henry's actions than even that most astute of long-term planners has foreseen. On the surface there are positive aspects to this conclusion: a play that began in war ends in peace, and it shows us the maturing of a king and his attempt to seal a bond with his people. Several of the books with which Shakespeare was familiar, *The Georgics*, *The Mirrour for Magistrates*, *The Boke of the Governour*, deal with man's constant awareness of what *ought* to be in the knowledge of what *is*, an unfading desire to narrow the gap between the real and the ideal, a gap which his age believed the fall introduced into the world as man yearns for the paradise he has lost. In the histories we are endlessly reminded that even in that country Gaunt calls 'This other Eden, demi-paradise' it is irrecoverably lost. As this Epilogue reminds us, men strive for and temporarily achieve peace and stability but it always gives place to further strife.

It is an appropriate conclusion to a play in which the constant yearnings for glory, brotherhood, the unclouded triumph of an ideal king, is balanced at every turn by fractious grumbling, cowardice, base self-interest and the dubious morality of political pragmatism. The irony may be pressed home forcibly, as it was in the Stratford, Ontario production of 1989. Amid a closing ball-room sequence Katharine came to represent France passed in an 'excuse-me' dance among various partners, from Henry to the Dauphin, to Clarence, and back to Henry. As the lights dimmed she was danced off into the darkness to leave Henry alone puzzled, staring at the ground as though he dimly foresaw some disaster in the future. This heavy foreshadowing overdid the irony Shakespeare offers. In the play the characters are sublimely confident in their success and their newly achieved unity, unable to see the ineluctable revolution of fortune's wheel. Amid the exuberance the Epilogue's chilling reminder gives us a perspective we do not have in our normal lives – that of history. Triumphant in politics and love at Troyes, Henry will soon be dead of dysentery. At the apogee things can only decline. Henry has emphasised, whenever it served his turn, his own mortality. It is the final irony that everything is lost because, as he says himself, 'the King is but a man as I am'. With each king the task begins again. Richard Levin (1975, p. 337) has objected to the kind of ironical reading, attached by critics he calls 'refuters', of Shakespeare's happy endings, which seek 'to persuade us that its author did not wish us to believe it'. But in this case the undercutting irony is in Shakespeare's own lines and is unavoidable for an audience which has experienced the catastrophes of Henry VI's reign across three earlier Shakespeare plays. Henry V, so skilled in the task of ruling, reigns only for nine years. Henry VI, left as a vulnerable child, the king Shakespeare shows to be the least fluent in political skills, is England's ruler for over forty years. He may be the most deeply religious of them all but it seems that God's vengeance falls on his reign. Henry V may be inscrutable in his actions to us but God's actions are inscrutable to Henry. In his cycle of history plays

Shakespeare repeatedly shows us how figures are torn down at the pinnacle of their power: Humphrey of Gloucester, Suffolk, Richard Plantagenet, Warwick, Queen Margaret, Hastings, Queen Elizabeth, Clarence, Buckingham, Lady Anne, Richard III in his first tetralogy; Richard II, Worcester, Northumberland, Hotspur and Falstaff in the second. In *Henry V*, figures expecting or enacting triumph as various as Cambridge, Scroop and Grey, the French nobles and Pistol are always in danger of falling, to use Richard III's phrase, 'Into the blind cave of eternal night'. Shakespeare reminds us, at the height of Henry's triumph, how soon this king would succumb to that danger.

The mixture of elements we observe in Henry, the man of the people and the man apart, should not surprise us, for the society around him contains such a mixture of elements. There are prelates eager to protect their power, noblemen hungry for glory, cowards who pretend to glory, dutiful officers, rogues in search of profit, and loyal soldiers. Henry pursues glory to secure his crown and all in the name of England's good. The audience is constantly aware that a case can be constructed against Henry but that his performance is so skilled that it cannot be conclusively proved, which, in politics, is how success is defined. Shakespeare begins to make us aware of a world in which 'Order is no more than a semblance of order, and the perfect king is that king who makes the greatest number of people believe he is the perfect king' (Manheim, 1973, p. 172).

We have often been reminded that the theatrical aspect of power was familiar to Shakespeare's contemporaries. Elizabeth told a deputation of Lords and Commons in 1586: 'We Princes are set on stages, in the sight and view of all the world duly observed.' In this play Shakespeare shows us how kingship operates as a constructed performance. We know that even when Henry appears to be a pleasant roistering madcap his behaviour is controlled by needs that go beyond personal loyalty. If he has to sacrifice a boon companion he will do so. Constantly vigilant to secure his political advantage Henry may be at different times, as it suits him, larger than life as a heroic leader, or an ordinary, mortal workman in his kingdom. In showing us the skill of Henry's performance Shakespeare provokes contant spasms of unease in us about it. The problem for the dramatist was how a king might maintain his grasp while coming to power without creating so many hostages to fortune that he would lose his crown. Richard II is a figure temperamentally suited to dramatise the loss of the crown. There is a touch of Richard II in Henry's soliloquy on the eve of Agincourt, but he does not allow an elegaic sense of loss and a crisis of personal identity to overwhelm him. Shakespeare implies that, to some degree, kings make their own luck. Richard earned Bolingbroke's challenge by his careless arrogance. That kind of challenge is brought up in the treason of Cambridge, Scroop and Grey which Henry contains and dismisses. We remember how the Gardener in *Richard II* had advised the necessary pruning of overripe saplings. Thereafter the only challenge from within the English camp is from Williams, which can be contained in a jest. Henry reconceives the role of king to avoid the kind of public self-dramatisation in which Richard II was a specialist. He has his private agonies, as his soliloquy shows, but they remain firmly private. He has none of the lachrymose self-torment Shakespeare had already exhibited in Henry VI, nor of that revelling in the split between public and private man which Richard III so enjoys. Henry designs his performance always for political ends rather than private pleasure and plays the game better than either Richard II or his father.

The stage history of the play is, ironically, a demonstration of a truth inherent in the play that men tend to make the world into what they wish it to be. So often the complexity of the play and its central truths were hidden, as actors and directors picked among the balance of juxtaposed ideas in the play and, by judicious cutting, emphasised only one side of them. What ought to be crystal clear about the play is that it does not need an editor to reshape its elements; it already has one striving to do that within the structure of the play – the Chorus. Many directors evidently still believe that Shakespeare did not know what he was doing and seek to help him by cutting and reshaping scenes to eliminate contradictions and jarring ironies. The play often ends up, like York's body at Agincourt, 'all haggled over'. Branagh's widely acclaimed film presented some of the countercurrents of the play to a large audience for the first time. It failed, however, to present anything like the variety Shakespeare offers. A film, of course, often provides an expansion in visual material in exchange for the play's text. It is worth remembering, nevertheless, that Branagh cut 53 per cent of the text and often in areas that were habitually cut before this century. The conspiratorial opening of the prelates (I.i) lost 80 per cent of its lines; the complex manoeuvring about the legal pretext for the war (I.ii) lost 65 per cent; 35 per cent of the king's speech threatening Harfleur was excised, as was 75 per cent of III.vii; all reference to the slaughter of the French prisoners was cut; 35 per cent of the pivotal scene, IV.i, was cut; IV.iv was entirely excised, as was all of v.i save Pistol's concluding soliloquy, and nearly half of the final scene (v.ii). In Shakespeare's play the Chorus strives to sweep us along, as patriotic reflex so often does, to stop us thinking, but much of what we see fails to validate that account. Branagh's film, like some recent stage versions, shows something of the juxtaposed material but we are still awaiting a production that will display the full range of the contradiction.

At the dawn of the modern political world Shakespeare fastens on the essential ambiguities involved in what a king, as a just, trustworthy shepherd of his people, must be, and projects an image of being, and the harsh, ruthless actions he may believe political necessity calls on him to perform. In an increasingly managed modern society we are often aware of how qualities of leadership become merely strategic constructions of promotional advertising. We know enough about the infighting required to achieve power to see that a certain ruthless toughness is an inescapable component of leadership. When we are shown too much of the manipulation we may fear that the integrity of the system is called into question. Shakespeare captures, in his transition from Richard II through Henry IV to Henry V, a variety of ways of situating a governing figure. The final play places the problem as sharply as it can be put in examining how power works, how it can be promoted to produce success. What it demonstrates, and Henry in his darkest moment acknowledges, is that he cannot ever be one of us. He comes closer and tries harder to project a bond of fellowship than either Richard II or Henry IV but, in the end, he remains the leader separate from us. It is a sacrifice we expect and may be thankful for in leaders even as we inevitably resent it. The play forces the irresolvable paradox on us, the cost to him and the cost to us. We recognise that Henry has uncommon skills in managing the role, and that we are wise to be wary of them. With Leontes we can say 'I have drunk and seen the spider'. For centuries, productions of the play simply drank deep on patriotism and refused to see the spider. If we respond to all of the play and its structure we cannot avoid the paradox of political leadership which Shakespeare explored throughout his career and nowhere better than in *Henry V*. Our politics continue to be plagued by the rarely achieved balance between the ideal and the real as we search for figures we hope can resist the taint of corruption and who can compel our conviction that they are pursuing our common welfare and have the pragmatic skills to attain it.

# Select Bibliography

Agate, James (1943), *Brief Chronicles: A survey of plays of Shakespeare and the Elizabethans in actual performance* (London: Jonathan Cape).

Allman, Eileen J. (1980), *Player-King and Adversary: Two faces of play in Shakespeare* (Baton Rouge: Louisiana State University Press).

Arden, John (1977), *To Present the Pretence* (London: Methuen).

Babula, William (1977), 'Whatever happened to Prince Hal? An essay on *Henry V*', *Shakespeare Survey*, 30, pp. 47–59.

Barton, Anne (1975), 'The King disguised: Shakespeare's *Henry V* and the Comical History', in *The Triple Bond: Plays mainly Shakespearian in performance*, ed. Joseph G. Price (University Park: Pennsylvania State University Press), pp. 92–117.

Beauman, Sally (ed.) (1976), *The Royal Shakespeare Company Production of 'Henry V'* (Oxford: Pergamon Press).

Berman, Ronald (ed.) (1968), *Twentieth Century Interpretations of 'Henry V'* (Englewood Cliffs, New Jersey: Prentice Hall).

Berry, Ralph (1977), *On Directing Shakespeare: Interviews with contemporary directors* (London and New York: Croom Helm).

Berry, Ralph (1981), *Changing Styles in Shakespeare* (London: Allen & Unwin).

Boaden, James (1825). *Memoirs of the Life of John Philip Kemble Esq.*, 2 vols. (London: Longman, Hurst, Rees, Orme and Green).

Bond, R. W. (ed.) (1902), *The Complete Works of John Lyly*, 3 vols. (Oxford: Clarendon Press).

Brennan, Anthony (1989), *Onstage and Offstage Worlds in Shakespeare's Plays* (London: Routledge).

Brewster, Dorothy (1913), *Aaron Hill, Poet, Dramatist, Projector* (New York: Columbia University Press).

Bullough, Geoffrey (ed.) (1962), *Narrative and Dramatic Sources of Shakespeare*, Vol.IV (London: Routledge & Kegan Paul; New York: Columbia University Press).

Candido, Joseph and Forker, Charles R. (eds) (1983), '*Henry V*': *An annotated bibliography* (New York: Garland).

Cole, John William (1859), *The Life and Theatrical Times of Charles Kean*, Vol.II (London: Richard Bentley).

Coleman, John (1886), *Memoirs of Samuel Phelps* (London: Remington).

Cook, Judith (1983), *Shakespeare's Players: A look at some of the major roles in Shakespeare and those who have played them* (London: Harrap).

Cooper, Roberta K. (1986), *The American Shakespeare Theatre 1955–1985* (Washington: Folger Shakespeare Library).

Crosse, Gordon (1952), *Shakespearean Playgoing 1890–1952* (London: A. R. Mowbray).

Cunliffe, J. W. (1916), 'The character of Henry V as Prince and King', in *Shakespearean Studies*, ed. Brander Matthews and A. H. Thorndike (New York: Columbia University Press), pp. 311–31.

Davies, Anthony (1988), *Filming Shakespeare's Plays* (Cambridge: Cambridge University Press).

Dean, Paul (1981), 'Chronicle and romance modes in *Henry V*', *Shakespeare Quarterly*, 32, pp. 18–29.

Dollimore, Jonathan and Sinfield, Alan (1985), 'History and ideology: the instance of *Henry V*', in *Alternative Shakespeares*, ed. John Drakakis (London: Methuen), pp. 206–27.

Foulkes, Richard (1988), 'Charles Calvert's *Henry V*', *Shakespeare Survey*, 41, pp. 22–34.

Frye, Dean (1965), 'The question of Shakespearean parody', *Essays in Criticism*, 15, pp. 22–6.

Geduld, Harry M. (1973), *Filmguide to 'Henry V*' (Bloomington,

Indiana: Indiana University Press).

Gilbert, Allan (1953), 'Patriotism and satire in *Henry V*', in *Shakespeare Studies*, ed. A. D. Matthews and C. M. Emery (Coral Gables, Florida: University of Miami Press), pp. 40–64.

Goddard, Harold C. (1951), *The Meaning of Shakespeare*, Vol. I (Chicago: University of Chicago Press).

Goldman, Michael (1972), *Shakespeare and the Energies of Drama* (Princeton: Princeton University Press).

Greenblatt, Stephen (1980), *Renaissance Self-Fashioning: From More to Shakespeare* (Chicago: University of Chicago Press).

Greenblatt, Stephen (1985), 'Invisible bullets: Renaissance authority and its subversion', in *Political Shakespeare*, ed. Jonathan Dollimore and Alan Sinfield (Ithaca, New York: Cornell University Press), pp. 18–47.

Gurr, Andrew (1977), 'Henry V and the Bees' Commonwealth', *Shakespeare Survey*, 30, pp. 61–72.

Hammond, Antony (1987), 'It must be your imagination then: the prologue and the plural text in *Henry V* and elsewhere', in *Fanned and Winnowed Opinions*, ed. John W. Mahon and Thomas A. Pendleton (New York: Methuen), pp. 133–50.

Hawkins, Sherman H. (1975), 'Virtue and kingship in Shakespeare's *Henry IV*', *English Literary Renaissance*, 5, pp. 313–43.

Hobday, C. H. (1968), 'Imagery and irony in *Henry V*', *Shakespeare Survey*, 21, pp. 100–11.

Hogan, Charles B. (1957), *Shakespeare in the Theatre 1701–1800*, Vol. II (Oxford: Clarendon Press ).

Holderness, Graham (1985), *Shakespeare's History* (Dublin: Gill & Macmillan).

Jackson, Russell and Smallwood, Robert (eds) (1988), *Players of Shakespeare 2* (Cambridge: Cambridge University Press).

Jorgensen, Paul (1956), *Shakespeare's Military World* (Berkeley: University of California Press).

Kelly, Henry A. (1970), *Divine Providence in the England of Shakespeare's Histories* (Cambridge, Mass.: Harvard University Press).

Kernan, Alvin B. (1970), 'The Henriad: Shakespeare's major history plays', in *Modern Shakespearean Criticism*, ed. Alvin B. Kernan (New York: Harcourt Brace and World), pp. 245–75.

Knight, G. Wilson (1958), *The Sovereign Flower* (London: Methuen).

Lee, Sidney (1906), *Shakespeare and the Modern Stage* (London: John Murray).

Levin, Richard (1975, 1977), 'Refuting Shakespeare's endings: Part 1', *Modern Philology*, 72, pp. 337–49; Part 2, *Modern Philology*, 75, pp. 132–58.

Manheim, Michael (1973), *The Weak King Dilemma in the Shakespearean History Play* (Syracuse: Syracuse University Press).

Merrix, Robert P. (1972), 'The Alexandrian allusion in Shakespeare's *Henry V*', *English Literary Renaissance*, 2, pp. 321–33.

Mosely, C. W. R. D. (1988), *Shakespeare's History Plays: 'Richard II' to 'Henry V', the making of a king* (Harmondsworth: Penguin).

Odell, G. C. D. (1966), *Shakespeare From Betterton To Irving*, Vol. 1 (New York: Dover).

Olivier, Laurence (1982), *Confessions of an Actor* (London: Weidenfeld & Nicolson).

Ornstein, Robert (1972), *A Kingdom for a Stage* (Cambridge, Mass.: Harvard University Press).

Patterson, Annabel (1988), 'Back by popular demand: the two versions of *Henry V*', *Renaissance Drama*, New Series XIX, pp. 29–62.

Quinn, Michael (1969), *Shakespeare: 'Henry V', a casebook* (London: Macmillan).

Rabkin, Norman (1977), 'Rabbits, ducks and *Henry V*', Shakespeare Quarterly, 28, pp. 279–96.

Rabkin, Norman (1981), *Shakespeare and the Problem of Meaning* (Chicago: University of Chicago Press).

Reese, M. M. (1961), *The Cease of Majesty* (London: Edward Arnold).

Ribner, Irving (1957), *The English History Play in the Age of Shakespeare* (Princeton: Princeton University Press).

Rossiter, A. P. (1961), *Angels with Horns*, ed. Graham Storey (London: Longmans, Green & Co.).

Rossiter, A. P. (1968), 'Ambivalence: the dialectic of the Histories', in *Twentieth Century Interpretations of 'Henry V'*, ed.

Ronald Berman (Englewood Cliffs, New Jersey: Prentice Hall), pp. 74–87.

Saloman, Brownell (1980), 'Thematic contraries and the dramaturgy of *Henry V*', *Shakespeare Quarterly*, 31, pp. 343–56.

Sanders, Wilbur (1968), *The Dramatist and the Received Idea* (Cambridge: Cambridge University Press).

Shakespeare, William (1773), *King Henry V*, ed. John Bell (London: printed for John Bell and C. Etherington).

Shakespeare, William (1947), *Henry V*. The New Cambridge edition by John Dover Wilson (Cambridge: Cambridge University Press).

Shakespeare, William (1951), *William Shakespeare: The complete works*, ed. Peter Alexander (London: Collins).

Shakespeare, William (1954), *Henry V*. The New Arden edition by J. H. Walter (London: Methuen).

Shakespeare, William (1966), *The Life of King Henry the Fifth*. The Pelican Shakespeare, ed. Alfred Harbage (Harmondsworth: Penguin).

Shakespeare, William (1968), *Henry V*. The New Penguin Shakespeare, ed. Arthur R. Humphreys (Harmondsworth: Penguin).

Shakespeare, William (1979), *Henry V*, ed. John Wilders (London: British Broadcasting Corporation).

Shakespeare, William (1982), *Henry V*. The Oxford Shakespeare, ed. Gary Taylor (Oxford: Oxford University Press).

Spanabel, Robert (1969), *A Stage History of 'Henry V'*, unpublished DD 69–22, 213 (University of Akron, Ohio).

Sprague, Arthur C. (1944), *Shakespeare and the Actors: The stage business in his plays, 1660–1905* (Cambridge, Mass.: Harvard University Press).

Sprague, Arthur C. (1964), *Shakespeare's Histories: Plays for the stage* (London: Society for Theatre Research).

Stribny, Zdenek (1964), '*Henry V* and history', in *Shakespeare in a Changing World*, ed. Arnold Kettle (New York: International Publishers), pp. 84–101.

Strype, John (1822), *The Life and Acts of John Whitgift*, Vol. 1 (London: Oxford University Press).

Taylor, Gary (1979), 'The text of *Henry V*: three studies', in Stanley Wells and Gary Taylor, *Modernizing Shakespeare's*

*Spelling, with Three Studies in the Text of 'Henry V'*, (Oxford: Oxford University Press), pp. 39–164.

Tillyard, E. M. W. (1962), *Shakespeare's History Plays* (Harmondsworth: Penguin).

Toliver, H. E. (1965), 'Falstaff, the Prince and the history play', *Shakespeare Quarterly*, 16, pp. 63–80.

Traversi, Derek (1956), *An Approach to Shakespeare* (New York: Doubleday).

Traversi, Derek (1957), *Shakespeare From 'Richard II' to 'Henry V'* (Stanford: Stanford University Press).

Trewin, J. C. (1964), *Shakespeare on the English Stage 1900–1964* (London: Barrie & Rockcliff).

Tydeman, William (1987), *'Henry V': A critical study* (Harmondsworth: Penguin).

Tynan, Kenneth (1967), *Tynan Right and Left* (London: Longmans).

Vickers, Brian (1968), *The Artistry of Shakespeare's Prose* (London: Methuen).

Wentersdorf, Karl P. (1976), 'The conspiracy of silence in *Henry V*', *Shakespeare Quarterly*, 27, pp. 264–87.

Winny, James (1968), *The Player King: A theme of Shakespeare's Histories* (London: Chatto & Windus).

# Index